09568904

understanding
Marx

Gill Hands

Hodder Education
338 Euston Road, London NW1 3BH.

Hodder Education is an Hachette UK company

First published in UK 2011 by Hodder Education.

This edition published 2011.

British Library Cataloguing in Publication Data: a catalogue record for
this title is available from the British Library.

10 9 8 7 6 5 4 3 2 1

www.hoddereducation.co.uk

Typeset by MPS Limited, a Macmillan Company.
Printed in Great Britain by CPI Cox & Wyman, Reading.

Contents

1

Marx's life and times

Karl Marx is sometimes known as the 'father of communism'. Although he did not invent the idea of communism he was the first person to develop the idea and write about it in a practical and scientific way. Marx believed in the ideal of a communist society; one where private property has been abolished and people live in equality, without classes or social divisions. This was a revolutionary idea in the nineteenth century and it brought Marx into conflict with the authorities in many European countries; it led to his exile to London and a life of relative poverty. He died in 1883 but it was not until the twentieth century that his ideas became widespread, led to revolution and the setting up of communist states. Marx wrote many articles and books throughout his life, the most well known are:

The *Communist Manifesto* – written between 1847 and 1848 with Friedrich Engels, Marx's closest friend.

Das Kapital – written between the 1850s and his death in 1883.

Europe at the time of Marx

Karl Marx was born on 5 May 1818 at Trier in the Rhineland, which was then a part of Prussia. Prussia was a large semi-feudal empire that covered what is known today as Germany and parts of Poland and Sweden. His father Heinrich Marx was a lawyer. Although the family was of the Jewish faith, Heinrich Marx registered as a Protestant Christian when laws were passed preventing Jews from holding public positions. This must have left some impression on Marx although he was never a devout religious believer.

The world that Marx lived in was very different from the Western Europe of today. In order to understand what Marx believed and why he believed it, we need to look at the society in which Marx lived and the influence it had on him.

Marx grew up at a time of rapid social change throughout Europe. The main forces for this change were:

* the Industrial Revolution, which had started in Britain. This led to the growth of the factory system throughout Europe and to an increase in the size and number of cities.
* the French Revolution of 1789 and the Napoleonic Wars (1799–1815), which led to the downfall of the monarchy and the abolition of feudalism throughout Europe.

Huge cities were growing up throughout the Western world, the invention of the steam engine and the growth of factories all meant that people lived in a completely different way to their ancestors. In the past, people had lived in close-knit communities and worked in traditional agriculture or as craftsmen. The rapid growth of the factory system meant that many independent craftsmen and small workshops disappeared.

Agricultural reforms and machinery increased the efficiency of farms and led to unemployment in rural areas. Landowners took over common lands and grazing rights that had belonged to the poor, increasing rural poverty.

The new cities and factory towns were soon flooded with destitute small farmers, craftsmen and their families. They were desperate to work under any conditions, living in slum housing and working long hours in factories or mines with unguarded and dangerous machinery. There were no safety regulations and even young children had to work.

Early life

Marx's upbringing was a middle class one. Little is known of his very early life as he became estranged from his family in later life. He came from a fairly large family with both brothers and sisters, but he was the oldest son and his brothers both died young. Young Karl was seen to be possessed of a strong and creative intelligence. He was fiercely independent, domineering and argumentative from an early age. It is thought that Marx was privately educated until he joined the Trier High School in 1830 at the age of 12. His school records do not show flashes of any particular genius but he showed signs of independent thought and of not going along with the crowd in his refusal to talk to a new state-appointed headmaster who was given a position at the school.

The old headmaster was a man of fairly liberal ideas and this led to a police raid on the school in 1832: literature in support of free speech was found circulating there and one of the schoolboy ringleaders was expelled. The headmaster was put under surveillance and eventually the authorities employed a very conservative co-headmaster to keep an eye on things. Marx would not talk to this man at all, and was one of the few boys who did not visit him after he graduated from school, much to his father's embarrassment.

Although intellectually powerful, Marx never had a particularly strong constitution and was dogged by ill health for most of his life. He had a weak chest, which led to him being found unfit for military service in 1836. His parents constantly fretted about his health when he went to the university of Bonn at the age of 17. They bombarded him with letters advising him not to study more than his health could bear, not to smoke, stay up late, drink too much wine and to keep his rooms and himself clean and hygienic.

He never took much notice of their advice and for most of his life he lived in a disordered way, smoked and drank far too much and spent long hours studying and writing.

University life

Marx followed in his father's footsteps and in 1835 he registered as a law student at the University of Bonn, although he later became more interested in history and philosophy. His academic career was rather erratic. He did not spend much time on his studies and became involved in a duelling society where he was injured above his right eye. His father insisted he should stop his 'wild rampaging' and move to a place with a more academic atmosphere.

In the autumn of 1836 he entered the University of Berlin, again with the intention of studying law. Berlin was a much bigger place than Bonn and the university had the reputation of being seriously academic and a centre of radical thought in the form of the 'Young Hegelians'. They were a group of academics, intellectuals and students who discussed and developed the ideas of the German philosopher Georg Wilhelm Friedrich Hegel (1770–1831).

Hegel had been the rector at the university and was almost an institution there. He was the nearest thing to an officially endorsed philosopher that existed, having been decorated by Frederick William III for services to the Prussian Empire. Most of his followers received appointments or preferment in the universities, for even these were controlled by the State. Hegel's philosophy is rather complex, but basically he believed that society progressed by intellectual development or 'Reason' and that Reason could be identified with a God-like figure he called the 'Absolute'. Hegel asserted that the Absolute had developed throughout history, but it had come to consciousness of itself and culminated its development in the state of Prussia. There was no further progress for it to make as it had reached its ideal.

The Young Hegelians agreed to some extent that the State should be the embodiment of Reason but they interpreted the theories of Hegel in increasingly radical ways. They saw the Absolute not as a God-like figure but as humanity itself. For a reader in the twenty-first century this does not seem particularly shocking but at the time the Church was a very powerful force in society. To suggest that mankind might be at the centre of the universe and not some God or Absolute was very daring. It was much later, in November 1859, that Charles Darwin made his theory of evolution public in *On the Origin of Species* and Friedrich Nietzsche (1844–1900), who saw that scientific discoveries had led to Western society becoming more secular and thought this might lead to a nihilistic viewpoint of a world without meaning, didn't proclaim 'God is Dead' until 1882.

Marx's association with these radicals meant that he could not obtain his degree in Berlin, especially as his thesis, on Greek philosophers Democritus and Epicurus, argued that philosophy should be detached from religion and freed from all kinds of dogma. It was finally accepted in 1841 at the University of Jena.

Life as a journalist

Marx hoped to take up a university teaching post after his studies, but because of his association with the Young Hegelians and other radical thinkers he was unsuccessful. He married Jenny von Westphalen in 1843. She was the beautiful young daughter of Baron von Westphalen, a cultured and progressive Prussian aristocrat. The baron had encouraged Marx in his childhood studies, advising him to read Greek poetry and Shakespeare.

In the same year Marx began to work for the radical paper *Rheinische Zeitung*. He was one of the first political journalists and his articles were some of the earliest examples of documentary reporting. He wrote several hard-hitting articles on the plight of peasants who had been persecuted for gathering firewood when common land passed into private ownership. Marx did not hesitate to criticize the government on this and other matters. This led to the paper being censored and Marx was eventually forced to resign. The paper was later closed down.

During his time at the paper Marx realized that his knowledge of economic and social matters was not very wide and he began to study political economy seriously. He saw that society was unfair and wished for change but he realized none of the current philosophies explained how the changes he wished for could come about. He felt that philosophy was not scientific enough and that philosophy in itself was not enough to change the world. Action would need to be taken!

In the autumn of 1843 he moved to Paris to escape restrictions imposed by the government in Prussia. Paris was the revolutionary capital of Europe with a large population of refugees including thousands of expatriate Germans. Dissidents were drawn in by the reputation of past revolutions, even though France was once again under the rule of a monarchy. It was here that Marx came into contact with communist and revolutionary sects, and mixed with people from all walks of life including artisans and workers. It totally changed the way he felt about society and the possibilities of communism. He worked on a new journal, the *German-French Annals*. Although it ran for only one issue because of distribution problems, it was important because it was the first time Marx had directed his appeals at workers rather than just intellectuals.

During his time at the paper Marx reacquainted himself with Friedrich Engels (1820–95) who was to become his lifelong friend and co-writer. Engels had been working as a business agent at his father's factory in Manchester, England where he saw the poverty and deprivation of the workers and wrote *The Condition of the Working Class in England*, condemning the society of the time. Marx was impressed and they soon became close friends.

Marx became more radical during his time in Paris and came under the influence of French and Russian anarchists, including Pierre-Joseph Proudhon and Mikhail Bakunin. Anarchists believe:

* society does not need government
* no government is legitimate unless consented to by all those it governs
* freedom is absolute. No one should be obliged to obey authority without freely consenting to do so.

These ideals became more important to Marx as he struggled to work out his own philosophy, although he later fell out with the anarchist leaders.

Marx and Engels became involved in the League of the Just, a revolutionary secret society with a large German membership. These expatriates were led by Wilhelm Weitling, a German tailor who agreed with Auguste Blanqui, a French extremist who believed in revolution. He thought that the majority of workers would not be won over to communism and a minority would have to seize power on their behalf. The League was banned in France and so the headquarters were based in London, where eventually a large split grew between those who believed the ideas of Weitling and those who believed that the workers could be won over gradually through education and that communism would evolve peacefully.

By 1847 Marx and Engels were in control of the League and had turned it from a secret society into an open organization called the Communist League. At the second meeting of the League in December, Marx and Engels were asked to draw up the statutes of the League and write a statement of principles, or manifesto. The League already had a slogan 'Working men of all countries, unite!'

The Communist Manifesto

The aim of the Communist League was to overthrow the old bourgeois society and Marx and Engels had to write some kind of document that would make their objectives clear. Unfortunately, Marx did not concentrate on the task straight away and it was only when he received a letter from the committee threatening 'that measures would be taken against him' if he didn't deliver the goods that he got on with it. It was finally finished in February 1848 and opens with the words: 'A spectre is haunting Europe – the spectre of communism.'

It is one of the earliest socialist writings and despite seeming dated and rather quaintly archaic in style it is still in print today and has some contemporary relevance. Although Marx had discussed the *Manifesto* with Engels and Engels had made several attempts at writing a version of it, the final document is almost entirely the work of Marx himself and it is here that Marxism can be seen in its embryonic form.

The *Communist Manifesto* was a statement of the principles of the Communist League, and was the first full statement of their world view. It described the unfair state of society and how it could be changed by revolution into an ideal communist state.

The *Communist Manifesto* was a document which:

* described the capitalist economy and how it came about – a capitalist system is one where there is private property and relatively free markets where goods are sold for profit
* described the proletariat or property-less working class, and how it was created
* examined the conflict between the proletariat and the middle classes, or bourgeoisie
* presented the objections others had to communism and criticized them
* put forward the idea of revolution and suggested how communism might work.

It contained the famous phrase, 'The proletarians have nothing to lose but their chains. They have a world to win. Working men of all countries unite!'

Because of his revolutionary ideas, Marx was becoming more of a threat to the established order. He was asked to leave several European countries because of his views, and was expelled from France in 1845, from Belgium in 1848 and exiled from Prussia in 1849.

Exile

Marx had already been exiled from Germany and from France and now that the *Communist Manifesto* had been published the Belgian authorities began to look on him with suspicion. The year 1848 was exciting for Marx and Engels, for not long after the *Manifesto* was published revolutions and uprisings began in many

European cities. King Louis Philippe abdicated in February 1848 as a result of the new unrest sweeping through France. A new French Republic was proclaimed. Could this be the start of the revolutions that Marx and Engels had hoped for?

Prussian police spies had been watching Marx; in April 1847 the Prussian ambassador in Brussels had demanded the suppression of the journal he was editing and now that uprisings had begun the authorities wanted him out of the country.

In March 1848, a decree signed by King Leopold I of Belgium ordered him out of the country never to return. Marx was not particularly upset by this as he had already considered returning to life in France. The official who had signed the form ordering his expulsion from Paris was now dismissed and Marx had been invited back by an old socialist comrade Ferdinand Flocon, who was now a member of the provisional government.

Despite his willingness to leave, he was arrested on trumped-up charges of not having a proper passport and thrown into a prison cell. Although this was the official reason for his imprisonment, it is likely that it had more to do with his funding of dissident Germans working in Belgium. Some of the money ended up being used to buy guns, knives and other weapons – no wonder the authorities were nervous. Jenny Marx was also imprisoned under very wide-reaching vagrancy laws and although both of them were acquitted by a jury the next day, they were given only a few hours to leave the country. They had to quickly sell all their possessions before being taken to the French border under police escort.

Marx arrived in Paris on 5 March and he and Engels, inspired by the French example, soon began working towards a German revolution. They amended the *Communist Manifesto* into *The Demands of the Communist Party in Germany* and distributed it as widely as they could.

Marx realized that he needed to be back in Germany in order to be more effective and so he decided to move back to Cologne. He still had contacts there and he hoped some of them would help in his new endeavour, a paper to be called *Neue Rheinische Zeitung*. When he arrived in Cologne he reported to the authorities and asked them to renew his Prussian citizenship but they refused. Engels returned to his family hoping that he could persuade them to finance this new venture but they did not.

Scraping together money, including Marx's family inheritance, they managed to publish the first issue in June 1848 and the paper soon had a large circulation. Some of this was due to the style of the paper, which was daring and often witty. In contrast to the other more dry and rambling philosophical German papers it was informative and came to the point. This did not go down well with the authorities as revolutionary uprisings were beginning throughout Germany and there were street fights in Berlin. A campaign of police harassment against the paper and its editors began. In October 1848 Engels left for Belgium where he was arrested and deported to France and the paper suspended publication for a few weeks.

When Engels returned, he and Marx were put on trial for 'insulting the public prosecutor'. No sooner did they get off this charge through Marx's brilliant and witty defence, than Marx was re-arrested on charges of 'incitement to revolt' for encouraging people to resist paying taxes, using force if necessary. Again, he was acquitted. Because he had been acquitted twice Marx began to feel that he was above the law and he still continued to write articles that upset the authorities and became even more daring. This was too much and the authorities pounced on the paper in May 1849, closed it down and prosecuted the workforce. All non-Prussians were to be deported and as Marx had not been able to get his citizenship renewed this included him. Everything was sold up, the family silver went into pawn and Marx and his family moved to Paris.

Paris was now totally changed from the city that he had left only recently. There had been a royalist reaction to the revolution and all foreign revolutionaries were to be evicted. Marx had hardly arrived when armed police came to the door to banish him to a rural part of Brittany; as Jenny was pregnant she was allowed another month to follow him. Marx did not wish to live in what he considered to be a swamp in the middle of nowhere. He could not go back to Germany or Belgium, he tried going to Switzerland but they wouldn't give him a passport, so he got on the next ship to Dover in England.

Life in London

When Marx came to live in London in August 1849 he only expected to be there for a few months at the most but he ended up living there until his death in 1883. London welcomed many refugees and was a place of sanctuary for many political dissidents. It was the largest city in the world at the time and there was a marked difference between the lives of the rich and the poor. The world of the poor was a sprawling industrial wilderness filled with factories spewing out smoke, sewers that poured into the River Thames, and slum housing where people crowded together in unhygienic conditions without clean drinking water or proper sanitation. Disease was rife, cholera epidemics were frequent and mortality rates were high. It was to this world that Marx brought his wife and children. Jenny Marx actually gave birth to seven children during their marriage but only three survived. It is alleged that Marx also had an illegitimate son by his wife's maid Helene.

His main source of income came from writing articles for papers such as *The New York Tribune*. Unfortunately he was unable to write in English at first and he relied on the help of Engels as translator. Engels was an excellent linguist – his friends said he could stammer in twelve languages!

Engels also helped by lending money to the Marx family who lived in extreme poverty when they arrived in London. Often they lived on nothing but bread and potatoes and three children died because of poor diet and lack of medicines; money even had to be borrowed for their funerals. Marx was a frequent visitor to the pawn shop where he pawned whatever he could, including his clothes. This way of life was especially difficult for his wife Jenny, who came from a wealthy background.

Nearly every day of his life in London Marx would turn up at the reading room of the British Library to work on his writing. He often stayed there for 12 hours and wrote again at home into the small hours of the morning. This was the writing which eventually became *Das Kapital*, or *Capital* as it is known in English. Volume one was finally finished in August 1867, but even then Marx continued revising and refining his work, making notes for the sequel he intended to publish. His letters are full of references to the toll that this work took on him. He was forever predicting that he was about to complete it but then finding he had more to write about.

Marx considered *Das Kapital* to be a scientific study of capitalism, politics and economics. He used the government Blue Books that were available at the Library to gather first-hand evidence on the plight of the poor. These contained statistics, census figures and reports from factory and public health inspectors. Engels had used these as a source for *The Condition of the Working Class in England*. Marx was impressed by this and decided to use them in a similar way in his masterwork.

Opinion is divided over the merits of *Das Kapital*. Many people find it a very difficult read. Marx was fond of satirical puns and he uses many literary references which are not easily understood by the general reader of today.

Marx also became known to more working people and activists through public speaking at working-men's clubs and political groups. However, he was fiercely argumentative and often quarrelled with members of the groups he worked with. He often publicly attacked those he did not agree with; for example, he wrote a criticism of the French philosopher Proudhon and got into a legal battle with Karl Vogt, a left-wing German politician. He was often seen in public life as bad tempered but in private he was a loving and gentle husband and father.

His final years were dogged by illness, especially bronchitis. He was a heavy smoker and often joked that the money he made from *Das Kapital* was not enough to pay for the tobacco he smoked while writing it. He also enjoyed drinking alcohol, sometimes to excess. Other illnesses were made worse by overwork. He spent a lot of time addressing meetings as well as writing his masterwork. A lot of his time was taken up by the International Working Men's

Association, or International as it became known; he was on the committee and wrote the constitution and inaugural address. The constitution was a daring statement at the time for the International members were pledged to subvert and possibly overthrow the existing capitalist regime by open political action. They were to do this by democratic means where possible by trying to enter parliament. Marx became a well-known figure in socialist circles and as the International grew rapidly the pressure of work began to take a toll on his health. In 1876 Marx requested that the council was transferred to America and eventually the original International fizzled out.

His wife died in 1881 and his beloved eldest daughter died a year later. Marx never really recovered from these deaths and he died himself in 1883. He was buried in Highgate Cemetery: only eleven mourners were at the grave and a short paragraph in *The Times* noted his passing. He was not well known or well respected, except in socialist circles, and few people believed that anything he said would have any effect on the world around them. Engels spent the next eleven years working on Marx's papers and completing the final volumes of *Das Kapital*. He died in 1895.

Marx's ideas spread around the world very slowly but became known to most of the world after the Russian revolution of 1917. Many revolutions have been started in the name of Marx but no country has ever had the truly communist society, where social classes cease to exist, that Marx hoped for. He is often seen as some kind of superhuman revolutionary figure who could do no wrong, though Marx himself often said his favourite motto was: 'I am a man and nothing human is alien to me.'

2

Marx and philosophy

Marx claimed to have little time for most of the philosophers who went before him. 'The philosophers have only interpreted the world in different ways; the point is to change it', he wrote in a thesis on Feuerbach, the German philosopher. This is sometimes seen as a statement that he was totally against the study of philosophy and saw it as a waste of time. In fact, he believed that philosophy should be made clearer by scientific study and then used to bring about social change.

The main debate among the philosophers of the time centred on two main schools of thought: Idealist philosophers, who assume there is a divine force of some kind that is responsible for the development of mankind; and Materialist philosophers, who believe that all ideas and beliefs come out of life and its conditions and not from any divine being or supernatural force.

It is easier to understand the importance of the debate and its relevance to Marx's ideas if we look at the development of Western philosophy up to the nineteenth century.

A brief history of philosophy

As philosophy tries to explain the truth behind life itself it must have been around for as long as humankind has existed. The earliest people had no means of recording what they believed so we can only surmise that they were superstitious and tried to explain natural phenomena as products of some divine force. Natural elements such as fire and water were worshipped as gods and from these beliefs organized religion developed.

In the Western world, the first philosophers (as we understand the term today) were the ancient Greeks, who started by criticizing religious beliefs. They used the scientific knowledge that was available to them at the time to explain the world around them and this sometimes brought them into conflict with organized religion and led to persecution.

The conflict between organized religion and free-thinkers went on for centuries. In Europe the dominance of the Christian church did not encourage the development of philosophical thought. Anyone who did not agree with orthodox Christian doctrines was likely to be branded as a heretic and tortured to death.

It was not until the fifteenth century that freer debate began, and it was not until the French and American Revolutions in the eighteenth century that the Church began to lose its dominance over the thoughts of the masses.

The materialist philosophers of the eighteenth and nineteenth centuries debated the existence of God and whether this could be proved by scientific means. Scientific development at that time was in the fields of mathematics and mechanical laws, for example Newton's Laws of Motion. This influenced the world view of the philosophers, who saw society as fixed and unchanging, believing it followed immutable scientific rules. It meant that people believed they had a fixed place in society that could not be altered. It was not until Hegel developed the idea of the dialectic that people began to understand that nothing was constant and that they themselves had a part to play in influencing the course of history.

Which philosophers influenced Marx?

Marx did not arrive at his own philosophy without studying, and being influenced by, those who went before him. He wrote, 'no credit is due to me for discovering the existence of classes ... nor yet the struggle between them'. Philosophers in the distant past, such as Aristotle, had seen the influence of class. Marx analysed the ideas of these ancient philosophers and read voraciously on many subjects. He also met many of the idealists and revolutionaries in Europe who wanted to change society. As he read and digested what they had to say, certain groups of thinkers became more important to him and became part of his own political and economic philosophy.

Ancient Greek philosophers

The study of ancient Greek philosophy was an important part of the education of young Europeans in Marx's time. It became even more popular in Germany under the influence of Hegel. There were three main ancient Greek influences on Marx's philosophy.

Democritus (c.460–c370 BC) was a Greek materialist philosopher who believed that the world could be explained by scientific laws, although science at the time was not advanced enough for him to be able to prove his theory.

Epicurus (341–271 BC) was a Greek philosopher who believed that if the world operates on mechanical principles then death and the gods are not to be feared. He thought this freedom from fear would allow people to live in peaceful communes devoted to pleasure.

Aristotle (384–322 BC) was a Greek philosopher, scientist and teacher. Aristotle saw the universe as fixed and unchanging and it was his view that was taken up by the official Church and dominated Western philosophy until after the Middle Ages. He was one of the first people to write that conflict in society often comes from economic conditions and inequality in the structure of society.

European philosophy

There are many philosophers in a great chain connected to each other through time, each building upon those who have gone before. Marx was influenced by reading many of the great Western philosophers.

René Descartes (1596–1650), a French philosopher and mathematician, was the father of modern philosophy. He believed that philosophy and knowledge could be unified and classified by mathematical means. This partly inspired the scientific method that Marx attempted to apply to his historical researches.

John Locke (1632–1704) was an English philosopher and physician. He believed that religion did not hold the absolute truth and that knowledge 'is founded on and ultimately derives from sense'. His belief in social equality – 'we are all equal, of the same species and condition ... with equal right to enjoy the fruits of nature' – and his belief that if the rulers of society offend against natural law they must be deposed, were to be a powerful influence on the American and French Revolutions.

Thomas Hobbes (1588–1679), an English philosopher and tutor, was one of the first people to try and study society scientifically in his book *Leviathan*, published in 1651. His view of society was an authoritarian one: he believed there should be an absolute ruler. He thought that people need a social structure, for life in a state of nature (i.e. before society exists) is 'solitary, poor, nasty, brutish and short'.

Utopian Socialists

Utopia was an imagined perfect place used as a literary device in a book by Thomas More (1478–1535). More did not think that Utopia might actually come to exist; for him it was a literary device that meant he had the freedom to discuss controversial and heretical ideas in an age of religious intolerance. The **Utopian Socialists**, on the other hand, really believed that their ideal societies could be built.

The Utopian Socialists lived and wrote at the beginning of the nineteenth century and observed the changes in society that were occurring around them. Many people at that time believed that industrialization and the factory system had led to changes in society for the worse. Following the ideas of Jean-Jacques Rousseau (1712–78), the French philosopher, such people wanted to return to some golden age in the past where life had been better. The Utopians disagreed: 'the golden age of the human race lies not behind but ahead of us', wrote Saint-Simon, one of the more well-known Utopians.

There was no specific movement that called itself Utopian Socialism – Marx and Engels were the first to use the term – but as the Utopian Socialists all lived around the same time and there are similarities in some of their ways of thinking it is valuable to consider them as a coherent group.

There were three major Utopian Socialists who influenced both Marx and Engels. They were not always clear about the way in which these societies would come into being, but they were all in agreement that the social structure of the time was unfair, riddled with inequality and needed to be changed.

Robert Owen (1771–1858) was a Welsh social reformer who believed character was formed by social conditions and that the greatest happiness of the greatest number should be the aim of society. He built model communities with schools and good housing for the workers in his mills.

Charles Fourier (1772–1837) was a French social theorist who believed society should be reorganized into self-sufficient units, or communes, with communal property and consumer co-operatives for the redistribution of wealth. It was his assertion that work should be made pleasurable and enjoyable so that it became physically and mentally satisfying. Society should try to eliminate all unpleasant jobs, learning to live without products and services that no one wanted to make or do. Fourier also believed that emotional ties were important, that people needed love and friendship as well as material possessions and satisfactions. In this way he was one of the first people to talk about the alienation that was later developed by Hegel and Marx.

Claude Henri de Saint-Simon (1760–1825) was a French aristocrat who narrowly avoided the guillotine during the French Revolution. This made him a fervent believer in social progress without the need for revolution. He welcomed capitalism because it would bring forward great scientific progress, which he believed was the key to the growth of society. Both Fourier and Owen saw capitalism and the Industrial Revolution as something evil that had changed society for the worse; their utopias were an attempt to make a type of rural, communal living popular. Saint-Simon, on the other hand, welcomed the technological changes that were happening and wished to exploit them. Saint-Simon's ideas are an important step in the development of Marxism because he was the first person to fully appreciate how industrial change had transformed society and to see it as part of the whole historical perspective.

Revolutionaries and anarchists

Marx lived at a time of revolution, The French Revolution (1789–99) had not long ended when Marx was born and this was a pivotal period in the history of Europe. After the revolution, French society and religion went through radical changes and the whole society was restructured. It was obvious that the age of the aristocrats was over and the citizens, including workers, were now a political force to be reckoned with. Marx came into contact with many revolutionaries; and anarchists, who believed in direct action by the masses and a rejection of all forms of government.

Louis Auguste Blanqui (1805–81) was a French revolutionary and extremist who believed in violent revolution and was the first to speak of the power of the proletariat.

Pierre-Joseph Proudhon (1809–65) was a French philosopher and economist, and the first person to call himself an anarchist. Proudhon rejected both capitalism and communism. He invented a form of anarchism called mutualism. Proudhon is famous for the saying 'property is theft'. This cry was taken up by revolutionary communists and is often wrongly attributed to Marx.

Louis Blanc (1811–82) was a French socialist and a leader of workers' groups who believed social equality should come about by democratic and peaceful means. His best-known saying, 'From each according to his ability, to each according to his needs', was another cry taken up by revolutionary communists and often wrongly attributed to Marx.

Mikhail Bakunin (1814–76) was a Russian anarchist leader who eventually came into conflict with Marx. He believed that communism was only the first step towards anarchism.

The importance of Hegel and Feuerbach

Marx was influenced by many different philosophers, thinkers and social reformers but the most important of them all was Hegel. Marx resisted Hegel's ideas when he first went to university but he soon converted to Hegel's philosophy, coming to reject most of it later when he developed his own ideas. However, even late in his life he said he was still indebted to the genius of Hegel.

Georg Wilhelm Friedrich Hegel (1770–1831)

Hegel was a German philosopher who believed civilization progressed through intellectual development and saw the history of society as a series of conflicts or 'dialectics'.

Hegel's philosophy is difficult to put into simple terms. It is often obscure and not related to the real world. Hegel's philosophical arguments have two main strands. The first is that human civilization comes about through intellectual and moral progress and that this is due to some kind of rational spirit that exists in humanity (universal mind) and not through divine intervention. He believed that civilization had been an intentional progression towards a fixed end, and that end was finalized in Prussian society in 1805.

The second strand is the development of the dialectic: that is the idea that change comes about as a result of conflict between two opposing movements. He saw this development consisting of three stages of dynamic movement, which are sometimes called thesis, antithesis and synthesis, although he rarely used these terms himself. According to Hegel, development happens in this way:

1 Thesis – the original idea or form is set up. This is also known as the 'position'.
2 Antithesis – the second, contradictory viewpoint contradicts the first. This is also known as 'negation of the position'.
3 Synthesis – the amalgamation of the two opposing views occurs. A 'negation of the negation' occurs but does not cancel it out, for a whole is formed. The whole is formed by overcoming the thesis and antithesis but still preserves them as a part of its final form. Hegel called this *Aufhebung*, which is sometimes translated as 'sublation'.

In Hegel's view, ideas develop through contradiction. The original idea, or thesis, is set up but is then contradicted and rejected by the antithesis. Eventually, the best parts of both the thesis and antithesis can be combined: this is called the synthesis. A synthesis of ideas cannot take place until the first two stages have been gone through. Because the synthesis is made from the amalgamation of two opposing viewpoints it also must eventually be opposed or rejected. A new idea will then take its place, to again be contradicted.

In Hegel's philosophy, ideas are constantly developing and changing and history progresses by learning from its mistakes. This contrasted with the beliefs of the materialist philosophers who went before: they believed that everything followed immutable natural laws, seeing man as a cog in a machine that he could not influence.

Marx later took this idea of the dialectic and applied it in a practical way to the development of society and the economy instead of to the purely philosophical world of ideas. He claimed that in Hegel's work the truth stood on its head and he had now put it the right way up by showing that ideas developed from the material world of economics; in other words, the conditions in which a person lives and works determine the way in which he thinks. This seems obvious to us today.

Ludwig Andreas Feuerbach (1804–72)

Feuerbach was a German philosopher and student of Hegel. In his most famous work, *The Essence of Christianity* (1841), he proposed that religion is 'the dream of the human mind'; in other words, man creates an illusory God based on human ideals and experiences. Feuerbach saw God as a projection of mankind's inner self and every aspect of God – morality, love, understanding, etc. – corresponds with the needs of human nature.

How did Marx differ from those who went before?

Hegel's ideas were important but Marx did not think they went far enough. Hegel believed that civilization had reached its final stage in the Prussian Empire and that there was no need for it to progress any further; he believed the State was the most important part of society. He accepted the political development and religious views within the Prussian Empire, so he believed that in any conflict between the State and the individual the State should prevail. He also held the rather contradictory view that human consciousness could achieve self-understanding and freedom. It was these apparent contradictions that were discussed by the Young Hegelians who, as we have seen, were instrumental in shaping Marx's philosophy.

Hegel said that people felt alienated from the world around them because of religious views that mean they are striving to live in an ideal world that they can only inhabit when they die. Feuerbach criticized religion and tried to show people that God was a creation of their own minds so that there was no need to feel alienated. Feuerbach felt that even Hegel's concept of a universal mind alienated people and that man himself was the centre of philosophy. He felt that the universal mind was a concept that prevented people from believing they could change their situation.

Where Marx differed from all these philosophers was his realization that it was not 'God' or 'Mind' that alienated people but money: 'Money is the alienated essence of man's labour and life ... it dominates him as he worships it.' It was then that he decided to devote his life to the study of economics and the way in which it affected social development. His development of historical materialism, a way of studying the ways in which the material world affects the world of ideas, came from his interest in Hegel's philosophy, but his own philosophy was also greatly influenced by his study of the great British political economists.

Political economy

When Marx started working as a journalist he began to read the works of the political economists in order to understand the practical realities of a world that he had little understanding of. They analysed and commented on the new form of trading and business that had affected the structure of society since the Industrial Revolution. There were two main political economists who influenced Marx.

Adam Smith (1723–90) believed it was natural for people to want to 'truck and barter' and so he believed the capitalist system could be justified as an extension of this natural need. Smith's ideas were an important part of the progress of political economy because he was the first to recognize that capitalists belonged to a class of their own. He also examined and described ideas of supply and demand which are now an important part of economic theory.

David Ricardo (1772–1823) wrote *On the Principles of Political Economy and Taxation* in 1817. Ricardo saw capitalist society as a natural thing but identified that there would be a class struggle over the division of profits in society.

What part did Engels play?

There is no doubt that Engels was an important figure in the life of Karl Marx; 'I owe it all to you, that this has been possible', Marx wrote in a letter to his friend. As the son of a wealthy manufacturer, Engels was able to support the Marx family financially, allowing

Marx to continue with his research and writing. However, there is great academic debate over the part he played in formulating Marx's philosophy. It is difficult for us to know now how much Engels actually contributed to the body of work Marx published during his lifetime.

Marx met Engels in Paris where they became great friends and co-writers and began collaborating on *The Holy Family*. This was intended to be a pamphlet exploring the class struggle but it eventually became a 300-page book. Engels only contributed 15 pages to the total. Other works on which they collaborated were *The German Ideology*, a criticism of the current German philosophy and the *Communist Manifesto*. Again we know from documentary evidence that Marx contributed most of the writing.

It is alleged that Engels wrote newspaper articles on behalf of Marx when Marx was too busy to do his own research. He also helped with translation and as an interpreter when Marx met foreign workers' leaders. Engels wrote mainly about science, business and industrial practice, of which he had first-hand experience from his father's textile mill in Manchester. He also specialized in writing on questions of war and nationalism.

It is well known that he completed the second and third volumes of *Das Kapital* from the unfinished manuscripts and notes that Marx left behind after his death. Marx was notorious for having bad handwriting and being badly organized so it was fortunate that the business-minded and efficient Engels was available to sort everything out. How much he altered the original manuscripts or put his own interpretation on the work is open to speculation.

When Marx died Engels became *the* well-known authority on communism and tried to keep all followers to the true path. He became the interpreter of all that Marx had said or written and kept up a huge correspondence until his death in 1895.

3

economic theory

In this chapter we look at Marx's economic analysis of capitalism. He examined the way that societies had changed throughout history and how this affected the economy. This is often known as 'historical materialism'.

His major work on the economy was *Das Kapital*. The first volume was finally published in 1867. There were three later volumes of his masterwork, which were published by Engels after Marx's death. His economic theories are also described in *Wage Labour and Capital*, and *Value, Price and Profit*.

The capitalist economy

Marx believed that there had been four main stages in the development of the economy and society up to and including capitalism:

Primitive communism – This was the type of society of primitive hunter-gatherers where people had to work in a co-operative way to benefit from the food and raw materials provided by nature. Marx saw this form of society as a classless one.

Slave society – This developed where some people gained power over others, usually as a result of warfare. There was a lower class of those that worked and were not free and an upper class that exploited them.

Feudalism – In feudalism the land was divided up between nobles in return for support for the ruler of the country. There was a strict class hierarchy from royalty at the top, down through nobles, clergy, merchants, guild artisans and serfs.

Capitalism – This is a form of society that developed after the French Revolution, which comprised two main classes: the bourgeoisie and the proletariat. The bourgeoisie were the rich and middle classes and the proletariat were the workers.

Under the feudal system, workers were tied to plots of land without rights. Their surplus products then became the property of an aristocratic landlord class. The capitalist system had a different economic structure because it relied on costly machinery and factories before products could be made. Only those with money to invest could afford to own these. Capitalism was unique because:

* only under capitalism does human labour power become a commodity to be bought or sold
* under capitalism all production is the production of commodities.

Commodities

The classical economist Adam Smith defined commodities as products that are produced to be sold on the market. Commodities existed before capitalism, as did money. However, under capitalism the economy is dominated by commodity production in a way that didn't exist in pre-capitalist society. In feudal or slave societies, a person would usually exchange a commodity to obtain something that they needed and money, if it was used, was just an intermediate stage of the process.

Theory of surplus value

At face value you make a profit if you sell something for more than you paid for it, but what makes one thing worth more than another, who decides it and how? Marx wanted to explore the question that puzzled the economists of the time: where does surplus value come from? To understand this he compared the way he believed the feudal economy worked with the workings of the economy under the capitalist mode of production.

Under the feudal system the landlord allowed his workers to cultivate the land in return for unpaid work, or rent, or both. It was obvious to all concerned that the landlord acquired the surplus product. Under capitalism this fact is hidden. Workers appear to be free to sell their labour power to the person who will give them the highest wages. It appears that they are given a fair day's wage for a day's work but, according to Marx, workers are being exploited. This exploitation is hidden by wages which allow the capitalist to cash in on the surplus produced by the workers. It took Marx many years to work out this theory of surplus value. It is a difficult concept, based on what a person's labour, or work, is actually worth and how it is exchanged for goods. To explain this it is necessary to go into detail about the way the capitalist economy works and it is more easily understood by going back to the basics of the economy as Marx did, starting with the labour theory of value.

The labour theory of value

All products in capitalism are commodities. According to Marx, commodities are valued in two different ways:

* **use-value** – This means a commodity has a value of 'usefulness' that meets the needs of the consumer. For example, shoes protect your feet, sugar will sweeten food, etc.

* **exchange-value** – This refers to the relationship between the different values of different commodities. For example, a barrel of wine may be worth ten barrels of fish, 50 kilos of sugar or ten pairs of shoes.

Use-values are not dependent on markets or any other system of exchange: sugar will always be useful for its sweetness. Exchange-values are dependent on market forces. A barrel of wine may be worth only 9 barrels of fish one week and 11 barrels of fish the following week. In order to understand how the capitalist makes his profit Marx first of all had to understand, and explain, the rates at which goods are exchanged against each other. What is it about ten pairs of shoes that makes them worth a barrel of wine? Marx believed it was the amount of labour that went into making the product that determined the exchange-value.

Labour must be applied to any commodity to give it use-value: someone would need to catch the fish, salt them and put them in a barrel; a cobbler would have to take leather and make it into shoes. This is what Marx called concrete labour. Each different commodity needs a different amount of concrete labour applied to it: shoes may take ten hours to make or it may take five hours to catch and salt a barrel full of fish.

Because the commodities need to be exchanged, they must have some kind of value in common, a way of working out what they are worth against each other. Marx called what they have in common their 'value'. The value is in the commodities because they are all products of human labour. Therefore, the exchange value of the goods can be worked out from the amount of labour that has gone into making the finished product.

If a cobbler spends ten hours making shoes and a fisherman takes five hours to collect a barrel of fish then a fair rate of exchange would be two barrels of fish to one pair of shoes. This is a very simple theory that doesn't take into account the cost of raw materials, the difficulty of the job or the skill of the worker. For example, an apprentice cobbler may take 20 hours to make a pair of shoes but this does not make the shoes more valuable. The labour theory of value depends on how much labour it takes to make a product on average or, as Marx called it, the 'socially necessary' labour time.

Money and capital

In a capitalist economy goods are not usually bartered or exchanged in this way. We use money to buy products from shops or markets. Money represents the value of goods and is a useful means of exchange. Money appeared in societies that existed before capitalism but not all money is capital. Capital is money that is taken into circulation in order to make more money. In Marxist terms capital is money to which surplus value accrues.

Marx puzzled over the way in which the capitalist was able to extract this surplus value; in other words, what is the means by which a capitalist makes his profit? If labour is a commodity then, like other commodities, it should be exchanged for its value. The capitalist who employs a worker for a day should pay, on average, the value of a day's labour, which will add the cost of a day's labour to the cost of producing the item. Following the exchange-value of labour theory, the capitalist can only sell or exchange the commodity at a rate of exchange corresponding to the value of the labour that was used to produce it. It would seem impossible for the capitalist to make a profit, so how does he do it? Marx worked out the solution to this problem which had puzzled many economists before him. The answer lies in the difference between labour and labour power.

Labour and labour power

A manufacturer of commodities needs to buy muscle power, strength and skill from the worker in order to produce goods over a period of time. This is labour power. It is a commodity with a value. If the value of a commodity is the amount of labour that goes into producing it, how much is labour power worth? Because labour power is the strength and skill of the worker then its value must be the value of the food, shelter, clothing, etc. that it takes to keep the worker in a fit condition to be able to work for a specific length of time. Labour is the actual work that is done – the activity that adds value to raw materials.

When a capitalist hires a worker his labour power becomes labour which belongs to the capitalist. The worker is paid for his labour power at an hourly rate but what he is actually giving is his labour. There is a difference between the value of the wage which the worker receives for his labour power and the value which is created by his labour. This is the surplus value which belongs to the capitalist.

Surplus value

Finally we get to the explanation of Marx's discovery: how the capitalist makes a profit from his workers. The capitalist pays the worker for a day's labour power and gains wealth because the worker always gets a fixed amount for his labour power regardless of the profit the capitalist makes from his labour. This is more easily understood by using an example.

If the cost of keeping a worker alive for a day is £1 and his working day is ten hours then the exchange value of ten hours labour is £10. In a factory a worker may be able to add £1 to the value of raw materials in eight hours. The worker has earned his wage in eight hours but the capitalist has bought ten hours of labour power so he is able to make a profit from the last two hours of the worker's day. This profit is multiplied by the number of workers in the factory. In effect the capitalist gets the use-value of the worker's labour power but pays only the exchange-value; the worker is getting a wage where the value is less than the value actually created by their labour. This could only occur because the capitalist economic system was unique in history: by historical and social accident the 'means of production' had come to be owned by one class, the bourgeois capitalists. This gave them the advantage over the workers who were virtually forced to sell labour on the open market in order to live. Their only alternative was to starve. In any society people have to do some kind of work in order to live, but it is only under capitalism that one class extracts surplus value in this way. In the long term this has an important relationship to the length of the working day.

Marx saw that the working day was divided into:

* necessary labour – the time the worker spends actually earning the amount paid in wages. In any society a worker would need to labour for a period of time in order to provide the food, clothing and shelter he requires. The amount of time this takes will vary according to the technology that is available to help him with his work
* surplus labour – the time spent producing surplus value for the capitalist.

The capitalist can increase his surplus value in two ways:

* make the working day longer
* increase efficiency in the workplace so the worker covers the cost of his wages in a shorter time. This means more of the rest of the day is available to produce surplus value.

Profit and the division of labour

The chief driving force in capitalism is profit. Not all the surplus value the capitalist gains from his workers is profit because he has had to pay for machinery, training, etc. The rate of profit the capitalist receives is variable and he is always looking for ways to improve it.

The capitalist system differs from past production methods by using a way of working called the division of labour. This is the use of mass production systems within the workplace so that a process is split into a number of repetitive tasks. A cobbler would have taken the leather through every process until he finished with a pair of shoes. In a factory, machines do the work in a number of different stages. One machine cuts the leather, one sews it, one shapes it, etc. This improves the capitalist's profits:

* One worker can do the work of several others. This will increase competition for jobs, so wages go down.
* It makes the work simple and unskilled so there is no need for long apprenticeships or training.
* Small-scale capitalists are put out of business because they cannot compete with the low prices of the large-scale manufacturers. They then have to join the workers.

However, this increased profit can only be gained in the short term. Once the capitalist's more efficient and improved production methods have spread to other manufacturers there will be an abundance of his product on the market. This is known as over-production and competition in the marketplace will eventually reduce the price of his commodity.

The capitalist can solve his problem in the short term by:

* exploiting old markets more efficiently, for example by advertising
* opening up new markets, for example by exporting to other countries.

Marx noted that there is always a tendency for the rate of profit to fall. Increased competition is one of the main factors in this because the capitalist finds he has to invest increasing amounts of capital into his business.

Following Marx's model it was generally believed that all modern economic crises would be as the result of over-production, but the global recession that began in 2007 included factors such as banking, investments and housing markets.

Capitalism in crisis

Marx believed that the capitalist structure of society would inevitably lead to crisis and internal contradictions would eventually lead to its downfall. The main problems that Marx predicted were:

* workers' wages will tend to fall to subsistence level
* profits will tend to fall
* competition will lead to large companies swallowing up small ones; this would be opposed by growing numbers of workers
* more people will be forced into the working class
* the capitalist system will lead to greater divisions in society
* there will be more and more severe economic crises
* capitalism has reduced workers to a degraded condition and these workers will eventually rise up in revolution and overthrow the system.

Falling wages and profits

Marx was convinced that capitalism was in crisis. Underpinning this belief was his faith in his dialectical analysis of the economy. He saw the whole of capitalism as inherently unstable because of the dialectical oppositions that made up its structure. If there was an economic 'boom' it was certain to be followed by a 'bust' or depression. He was also convinced that wages would become lower and lower until they reached subsistence level and that profits would keep falling because in capitalism the price of goods, and the profits made, are dependent to a great extent on the markets and on wages:

* high wages for workers lead to high prices for commodities, therefore factory owners get low profits
* low wages for workers mean that they are unable to buy enough goods and services to keep the economy viable and this leads to unemployment.

Social labour

Another problem affecting profits in a capitalist society is that nobody decides who is going to make what. We saw that use-value is an important part of Marx's economic theory. The products made have to be 'useful' for some human need. But they also have to be useful for some specific need, in a specific place: for example, if you are hungry you cannot eat a pair of shoes. In order for society to function we need all different kinds of commodities. If everyone decides to make shoes, for example, we will all go hungry. So societies need to have some way of regulating who makes what to ensure that enough of the right kinds of commodities are made.

Marx called this social production and he pointed out that the capitalist system was unlike slave or feudal societies in this respect as there is no way of making sure this happens. To a great extent, in slave or feudal societies the slave owner or the landowner decided the distribution of labour. They decided what they wanted and who would make it so that it met their needs. In a feudal society, with rural industry, the families who made up the society further regulated the distribution of labour. Some members would grow grain, some would weave, some would make shoes and the labour would be distributed so that it was relevant to age, sex, the seasons of the year, etc. They would be producing commodities that they needed and that they had to provide specifically for those above them in the ruling classes.

Capitalism, however, is a system of generalized commodity production. Factories are specialized and tend to produce only one kind of product. No producer can meet all his needs from the products of his own factory so he has to sell them as commodities to other people. In this way commodity producers are interdependent on each other.

Because there is no system of regulating who makes what, apart from market forces, this can lead to problems:

* It is not possible to tell if the products will be 'useful' until they go onto the market. The producer might not be able to sell them. In that case, according to Marx, the labour that

has gone into such products is therefore not social labour because it has been wasted. The goods are of no use to society.

* Manufacturers often compete for the same markets by making very similar products. The most successful will be those who can make them cheaply. Manufacturers can only do this effectively by increasing productivity and undercutting one another.

Manufacturers do not know whether or not their products will fill a social need in advance and can only determine this by trying to sell them. Because they are interdependent on each other and in competition at the same time this must lead to market fluctuations.

We saw earlier in the chapter that the price of commodities depends on the amount of 'socially necessary' labour time that goes into making them. In the marketplace of generalized commodity production it is difficult to see how much socially necessary labour time goes into making a product. To take the example used earlier, there is no easy way of telling that a fair rate of exchange of products is two barrels of fish to one pair of shoes. Competition between manufacturers and the way that surplus value is extracted means that labour has become abstract social labour and related to money. This is related to the 'fetishism of commodities', which is discussed in the next chapter.

Accumulation and crisis

We have seen that in a capitalist economy surplus value is acquired from the workers and becomes a profit. This is not often used by the capitalist to buy another product but is invested in further production. So surplus value goes into producing more surplus value. Marx called this the accumulation of capital and he believed it became almost an obsession for the capitalist.

Marx realized that investment of capital is important to the growth of the economy; capitalists have to plough back parts of their profit into the economy otherwise it will stagnate.

However, as the markets are not controlled in any way, if the capitalist cannot sell his product because there is no demand, or if supply exceeds demand, there will be a slump. In this case people tend to hoard money rather than reinvest it because profits become very low. This makes the slump even greater. Large amounts of commodities will remain unsold and so the capitalist will not get a profit from his investment. This is a crisis of over-production, which Marx said was unique to capitalism. Under the feudal system economic crises were usually the result of not enough being produced, leading to famine.

Centralization of the economy

Because Marx saw the competition between rival capitalists as one of the main economic problems, he believed that the economy should be managed centrally:

* Important industries should be centralized, only useful goods and services should be produced and over-production should stop.
* Banks should be centralized. It is only in this way that society can be sure there would be high levels of investment in the right kind of industries.
* There should be controls on imports to help combat unemployment.

Marx believed that these measures could only work in the communist society that would inevitably come about as a result of inconsistencies within the capitalist system.

Was Marx right about the economy?

There is no doubt that capitalism has gone through repeated crises since it began. There was the Long Depression in the 1870s and 1880s, and the Great Depression of the 1930s affected most of the capitalist world. At the beginning of the twenty-first century there was a world economic boom, followed by a global financial crisis beginning in 2007. More crises are being predicted, but how much all these crises are a result of the dialectic flaws inherent in capitalism is open to debate.

Modern neo-classical economists, such as those academics who follow the ideas of the Chicago School, would argue that boom and bust in the economy are just a part of the natural cycle of the economy. They reject the idea of dialectical instability and believe that market economies are inherently stable if left to their own devices. They believe that government intervention is the cause of depressions. They disagree with the assertion that labour is the only source of value in the economy and the only way of making a profit. Radical Marxists view these arguments with suspicion and say that as the present dominant view of the economic system in the West is a neo-classical one, stressing free enterprise, then it is in the interests of economists to support a system that benefits them.

Marx never finished his work on the economy. Volume 1 of *Das Kapital* was the only volume he completed so he did not really have time to formulate his theories properly before his death. Because Marx's views changed throughout his lifetime, there is a lot of discussion about which of his writings should be taken into account when stating his view of the economy.

The predictions that Marx made about the economy have not all come about: profits do not tend to fall, workers' wages have improved in real terms and the majority of people are much better off than they were in Marx's day. For the majority of people in society, class divisions have become less distinct. Where communists have come to power through revolutions their economies have suffered just as many economic crises as capitalist countries, although for different reasons. However, we have seen the takeover of smaller companies by large ones and several depressions in the economy with periods of high unemployment, so Marx was not totally wrong; and although economists try to predict the future of the economy, they cannot really know what will happen next.

4

economy
and
society

For Marx, economics did not exist in a vacuum, as a subject to be studied for its own sake. He was interested in the way that the economic structure of society affected the lives of the people within it. Capitalist society had developed fairly gradually in Europe, but in the second half of the nineteenth century it had started to develop very rapidly along with technological change. Marx saw that this had very definite effects on the lives of both rich and poor. He also saw that the effects of a capitalist economy were starting to be felt around the world and not just in the countries which had developed their means of production.

Imperialism and colonialism

Marx did not publish any theory of imperialism, although he did make reference to colonialism in the first volume of *Das Kapital*. Imperialism and colonialism are sometimes used interchangeably as words to explain the policy of one country extending control or authority over other countries outside its own borders. Colonialism is usually seen as rule over colonies that 'belong' in some way to the ruling power, for whatever reason. For example, India was at one time a British colony.

Marxists today use the term imperialism in a slightly different way from that used in a historical sense. The generally understood term describes imperialism as a policy of extending authority over foreign countries by acquiring and maintaining empires. Marxists see imperialism as the state of capitalism that takes place when colonialism has taken over the world.

This definition of imperialism comes mainly from Lenin's work *Imperialism: The Highest Stage of Capitalism*. Here he states that once all underdeveloped countries have become colonies of more developed ones there will be no new colonies available to be acquired by the major powers, unless they take them from each other. He also claims that capital will be concentrated in the 'financial oligarchy'; banking and finance will be dominant over industrial capital.

Imperialism is also a term much used by modern Marxists to describe the capitalist system of trade and banking and it is often used as a disparaging term to describe a greater power acting at the expense of a lesser power, regardless of whether or not the greater power has any rule over the lesser power. For example, the United States is sometimes referred to as the 'American Empire' because it is the dominant economic and military power in the world, even though it does not possess an actual physical empire.

What all these definitions of imperialism have in common is that some form of exploitation is taking place. Imperialists are often criticized for economic exploitation. The dominating power often makes use of other countries as sources of cheap labour and raw materials and as markets for manufactured goods they have produced. The concept of imperialism amounting to exploitation can be traced back to Marx's original thinking on the subject of colonialism.

Historians divide imperialism into periods of time or epochs:

* **Mercantile capitalism** – This is the first stage of imperialism. It began in the sixteenth century when explorers discovered new continents and plundered them. Large companies became the governing power in countries where they settled.

* **Colonialism** – This is the second stage of imperialism. Capitalist countries took over governing power from the companies set up under mercantile capitalism. Where the local population would not accept this rule, armed force was used.

Marx saw the globalization of capitalism as inevitable. He believed profits under capitalism would fall and that one short-term way of slowing down the rate at which profits fell was by opening up new markets. This meant the capitalists had to export their goods into other countries. Colonialism meant there were excellent protected markets for manufactured goods. Even where former colonies became self-governing countries, such as Australia, they often had economic and trade agreements that meant they were still dependent on Britain.

In the early nineteenth century Britain was really the only fully industrialized nation and was known as 'the workshop of the world' as it produced about 30 per cent of global industrial output. By the end of the nineteenth century other European states and the USA were able to enter the world of capitalist exporters. They made things very efficiently and flooded the world markets with cheap goods that meant they could undercut any of the opposition. The markets for these cheap goods were often developed at the expense of local industries.

Capitalism could not develop in these countries at the early stages of their exploitation as they were deliberately held back from any form of development. It was only later, at the beginning of the twentieth century, that the capitalist system itself began to be exported. There was investment in the employment of industrial workers in the colonies, but only when this did not interfere with industries in Britain and the other imperialist states. This was mainly in industries that were fairly close to the raw materials: mining, food processing, etc. At this stage in history there was also a huge scramble for power between European nations over the African continent. Some modern Marxists believe these factors created the Developing World, or Third World as it is sometimes known, and the current stage of imperialism: neo-colonialism.

Marx believed that revolution would only take place on a worldwide scale after the capitalist system had been exported. He was convinced that revolution could only take place if societies had developed to the stage of capitalism with the class divisions of bourgeoisie and proletariat, for it was the proletariat who would start the revolution. The revolutionary process would have two stages:

* Firstly, there would be a bourgeois revolution against imperialism.
* Secondly, there would be a revolution of the proletariat against the bourgeoisie.

Marx was not a trained economist and although globalization of the capitalist system did occur it was not entirely in the way that he predicted. He saw the world economic situation in a rather simple way and in reality the colonies had very different social structures that he did not entirely take into account. Communist revolutions did take place in some former colonies, but Marx's words were often distorted to fit the requirements of anybody who wished to see a change in the political system in their country. A truly communist society, without classes, was never the result.

Fetishism

In primitive societies, and in some kinds of religion, inanimate objects are sometimes thought to have supernatural powers (for example, voodoo dolls or holy statues). In capitalist societies people suffer from the illusion that inanimate money or commodities also have powers and properties of their own. A fetish is an object of desire, worship or obsessive concern. Marx saw three types of fetishism in capitalist society:

* fetishism of money
* fetishism of capital
* fetishism of commodities.

Money fetishism

Throughout history money has always had an element of fetishism about it, especially when it was in the form of precious metals, gold in particular. Seventeenth and eighteenth century European merchants were obsessed with gold and silver and believed that possession of large quantities of precious metals would be enough to let a country win a war. However, gold in itself is worthless. If you have ever read the book *Treasure Island* by R. L. Stevenson you will remember the character Ben Gunn, who was marooned on a desert island with a treasure chest. The treasure was of no use to him because he could not use it to buy anything and what he really desired was a little bit of cheese. Money fetishism is an illusion that deceives workers, making them think of money as the goal of their labours and thinking of their worth in terms of money.

Capital fetishism

This is the belief that capital in itself is valuable and that it does not owe anything to the labour that goes to produce it. Marx argued that capitalists felt that increased productivity was due to the capital they invested in their business and not the labour of the workers. Capitalists also feel that their money is productive when it is in a bank earning interest. Although it is making them a profit, it is not actually producing anything.

Commodity fetishism

One of the great points of controversy among Marxists and academics is the idea of commodity fetishism. This is possibly because Marx did not write very clearly on the subject and the idea seems a rather abstract one. At one level Marx seems to be saying that because the capitalist is exploiting the worker there is a hidden aspect to the real value of a commodity that nobody is aware of, that there is a veil of secrecy over the true worth of the products we buy. A modern-day example of this would be 'designer labels', where goods that are produced cheaply in developing countries sell at vastly inflated prices because of some false idea of their worth. It is very difficult for the buyer to know what the materials cost, who made them, how much the workers were paid, etc.

At another level is the belief that some commodities have a kind of intrinsic value that makes them more valuable than others and is not related to their exchange-value. For example, some commodities, such as holy statues, appear to have magical properties that make us blind as to their real value and so we become alienated. This is a more difficult argument to understand and some Marxist critics believe it is an interpretation that Marx did not intend in his original writing. Whatever interpretation is placed on the idea of fetishism, it is clear that Marx believed that under capitalism people experience social relations as value relations between things and that this causes alienation. We can take the example of the pair of shoes again and look at the idea in a less abstract way.

A woman might desire an expensive pair of shoes she sees in a shop and will work to have enough money to buy those shoes. In a capitalist society the money and shoes are independent from each other in a social sense. The people who made the shoes and the woman buying them are not aware of each other or of any social relationship between them. Marx believed that this caused alienation in society, because we are not in immediate relation to the products we buy. This then leads to a vicious circle where people believe they can relieve the alienation they feel by buying more consumer items.

The idea of commodity fetishism is strongly reliant on the labour theory of value and the concepts of exploitation and alienation, so critics of those concepts criticize fetishism as well. Marx believed that all three kinds of fetishism were features of capitalist society that stopped people from understanding and changing society. They are illusions that play a part in the alienation of humans under capitalism.

Alienation

Marx wrote a great deal about alienation and it is one of the areas of his thought that is still acknowledged as having great relevance today. Most of us are familiar with the term 'alienation' today: a sense of feeling outside society, or estranged from it.

The Marxist sense of alienation is more complex than this. For Marx alienation is not just a feeling or philosophical concept but an actual, concrete thing: a state of being that is a result of living in a capitalist society. To understand this we need to look at the way Marx views humanity and society.

Most of Marx's early work shows a great debt to Hegel's theory of alienation, and its development by Feuerbach. Hegel had shown that people were alienated but believed it was due to their yearning to be part of the universal mind. Alienation for him was a religious concept. People naturally yearn to have what they perceive as a unifying and spiritual essence within themselves. Most religions (and we have to remember that Hegel was talking mainly about Western religion) say this can only be achieved by a supernatural being that lives outside the real world, and the only way humans can achieve this is by merging with this being at some level, usually after death. Hegel believed this led to a kind of false consciousness where people believe they are separate from the divine or opposed to it in some way. Feuerbach saw alienation in less mystical terms for he believed that 'God' was not outside us but a product of the human mind. The values we attribute to God are those that we ourselves possess but we project them onto God. In this way, we become alienated from ourselves. Feuerbach believed that if people could free themselves from religious illusion then they would be able to live in harmony with each other and with their own true nature.

Marx saw alienation in practical, economic terms and for him it is not even necessary for a person to feel alienated to be alienated: it comes as a result of living in a capitalist society. In order to understand why he believed this we need to look at the way Marx perceived the human condition. Marx did not see human nature as an abstract and unchanging thing as the philosophers before him had done. After studying the economics of society in historical context he saw human nature as a product of social relations. His historical materialism gave him the view that human nature is in a constant process of development, and that as societies change so do the needs of the people in them. In his writings he talks of the 'species being', which is the essence of humanity and a development of the ideas of Feuerbach.

Marx believed that 'labour is the essence of man' and that people are labouring creatures; humans are basically producers and being able to work in purposeful creative activity brings us contentment. In this way we might be seen to be similar to ants or bees, but for Marx we differ greatly from them because we possess consciousness. Marx saw that humans, like animals, are a part of nature; we have similar needs for food, shelter and a desire to reproduce our species, but our consciousness means we are aware of what we are doing. We are aware of who we are and we see ourselves in relation to the rest of our species. This is important, for unless we are conscious of these things in the first place we cannot feel alienated from them. In fact some existentialist philosophers would maintain that it is precisely because we are self-conscious that we feel alienated; they argue that it is part of the human condition and it would not matter what kind of society we lived in. Marx did not believe it was only consciousness that distinguishes us from animals and he develops this idea in *The German Ideology*. Meaningful work is important to all humans. For Marx, labour is an important part of social development and fundamental to human beings, for through it we change nature and society and in the process we change our selves.

The opposite of alienation is actualization, or affirmation of the self, which Marx believed humans achieved from the purposeful use of their consciousness. He did not believe that work was supposed to be drudgery to be done away with, as many of the

Utopian Socialists believed. Work is an integral part of humanity and unless people are in right relation to it then they will be alienated; according to Marx, labour is essential to the 'species being' of man but the new capitalist system changed the ways that people worked so that they were not in a 'right relation' to their labour. The factory system, and the society that had grown up around that, had perverted the natural relations of people to the products of their labour and to each other.

The capitalist system of working alienates all those in it, both rich and poor. Workers are alienated from the products they make because they do not benefit from them. 'Labour produces fabulous things for the rich but misery for the poor', Marx wrote in *The Economic and Philosophic Manuscripts*.

Workers are alienated and de-personalized by the capitalist system because of the way in which the capitalist obtains surplus value from their labour. The capitalist system also means that they are told when to work, how to work and they derive very little personal satisfaction from their labours.

The environment of some parts of the capitalist system, the factory system, is dehumanizing: it is hostile to the workers and physically and mentally damaging to them. The constant repetitive nature of the work is not harmonious with human nature. The division of labour and the way the factory system is set up is also not natural, according to Marx, because it encourages competition instead of co-operation and it alienates people from each other.

Exploitation

Alienation is connected to exploitation by the capitalist. Marx saw the exploitation of one class by another as a fundamental part of an industrialized capitalist society. Marx believed that there had always been exploitation but it was only under the capitalist system that exploiting others became the normal way of working. In Chapter 3 we saw that the capitalists hold the balance of power. They are able to make a profit from the surplus value because they own the means of production. The worker is not aware of the fact that he is being exploited. He believes the capitalist has a right to the surplus value that is produced because he believes that is just the way things are, or part of human nature. This kind of exploitation is not really visible, unlike the more common forms of exploitation such as making people work long hours, child labour and difficult and dangerous working practices and conditions.

In the introduction to *Das Kapital* Marx says that he has not painted a picture of capitalists and landlords in a 'rosy light'. There are many examples of explicit exploitation of workers given as examples in the book. Chapter 10, The Working Day, consists of mountains of evidence that Marx collected from reports and newspaper articles. Evidence includes children working in mines and heavy industry in appalling conditions, engine drivers working 21-hour shifts, and dressmakers and milliners forced to work in overcrowded sweatshops where they died of consumption. Capital is 'vampire like', writes Marx in the introduction, and it 'sucks living labour'.

In the Victorian era the average age of death among the working classes was just 19 years old. Marx records descriptions of the physical state of many of the workers in British industrial cities in *Das Kapital*; many of the examining doctors report on the undernourished and progressively stunted growth of the working class.

Marx believed that a shorter working day would greatly benefit those people and in most democratic countries today there are laws to regulate the hours that people have to work. The workers who had to fight for improvements in working conditions by uniting against the capitalists found their inspiration in the works of Marx.

Marx applauded those who did their best to alleviate working conditions but he believed that both worker and capitalist alike are victims of the system. The capitalist is only a part of the society around him and has no choice but to continue with things the way they are, for even if a factory owner were to give away his goods and his factory somebody else would take his place. He saw capitalism as a great civilizing influence but believed it was only a part of the progression of history and not the final stage of development as others at the time believed. Marx thought that it would give way to communism and that it is only under a communist system that there would be no exploitation of any kind. He believed this society would only come about when people become aware of the true nature of society and their alienation.

Marx believed that capitalism seduces consumers by giving them desires which enslave them. The goods that a worker produces eventually enslave him because he is trapped in a cycle of working for money to buy goods; fetishism of goods means that people want to buy and consume more. The fetishism of money means that people have to sell themselves to obtain it and then desire money for its own sake. Private property also alienates people because they believe that an object only has worth if they can possess or use it. Marx even went so far as to say that people do not appreciate objects for their aesthetic beauty but only in relation to their commercial value.

Marx believed that even capitalists are alienated but they are 'happy in their alienation'. Their power, wealth and privilege are substitutes for true happiness.

On the other hand, the alienation of the workers is oppressive. They are the ones who truly suffer from alienation as they have nothing – neither the means of production nor the end products. All they hold is their labour power. The capitalist cannot exist without the worker; the worker believes he cannot survive without the capitalist because of the hold that money and wage labour have over him. In *The German Ideology* Marx describes how the abolition of private property and regulation of labour would abolish alienation between them and their products and would let them be in control of their lives again. Marx believed that realization of alienation was a vital step towards the revolution that would bring about communism. Capitalism was in crisis due to its internal conflicts, and it would go through a series of crises that would bring it to its knees. Once the workers understood their alienation and exploitation they would rise up and help to finish it off. A revolution would take place.

5

class, class struggle and revolution

Long before Marx, historians had discovered the existence of social classes, but class awareness and classification became more important in Europe at the end of the eighteenth century as a result of the French Revolution. Marx did not define class in any of his works and used the term rather loosely to mean different things at different times, but he believed that class is defined purely by economic factors. He saw that classes are made up of individuals who share a common relationship with the means of production. At the time he was writing, he saw that the capitalist economy had divided society into two opposing camps:

Bourgeoisie: the class of capitalists. Owners of the means of production and employers of wage labourers.

Proletariat: workers who have no capital or means of production of their own. They are reduced to selling their labour power in order to live.

Marx believed a scientific study of the ways in which society had developed would help prepare the working classes to overthrow the system by showing them the historical perspective of their position. He believed that capitalism was the latest form of exploitation in a series of oppressive rules throughout history and that if people were shown this then they could be persuaded to take action against their oppressors. It was only in this way that a classless communist society would eventually come about.

The development of capitalist society

In the earliest societies, when people lived as hunter-gatherers and small-scale farmers, there were no real classes. Society was organized on the basis of common labour and mutual protection and there was no private property. People scratched out an existence at subsistence level and had just enough food for basic survival. In Marxist theory this type of society is known as 'primitive communism'.

As societies became more efficient in producing food, the surplus products often came under the control of a ruling elite. The surplus products allowed the ruling elite to live off the labour of those below them in the class structure without having to produce anything themselves. This elite was often only a minority of the society as a whole. Throughout history the ruling elite has changed: slave owners, religious leaders of many types, feudal lords and, finally, capitalists. In the *Communist Manifesto*, Marx and Engels defined capitalists as the owners of the means of production and the employers of wage labourers. Because the factory system that sprang up after the Industrial Revolution was based on the purchase of large items of machinery, it was only a minority of the population who could afford to invest in it, so they became the new ruling elite.

Dialectical materialism and class structure

Marx saw history as a series of dialectical conflicts. Each type of society, whether based on slavery, feudalism or capitalism, contains contradictions inside its structure which can only be expressed through conflict. These conflicts will eventually lead to the downfall of the system. A new system will then take its place. Marx said this had been demonstrated throughout history.

In the original hunter-gatherer societies there was no real division of labour; everybody could do any job that needed to be done and could use any of the tools that were available. These societies were classless in a Marxist sense, but then they developed into slave-owning societies which became unstable and collapsed due to internal contradictions. The ownership of slaves was dependent on warfare, which put pressure on the economy. Eventually, this undermined the power of the state, allowing barbarian invasion, which then led to the collapse of the system.

Feudalism replaced slavery in Europe and it allowed people to develop skills and talents under the patronage of the landed nobility. However, feudalism was eventually overthrown by revolutionary struggles which continued into the nineteenth century when the rise of capitalism began.

Capitalism was necessary to allow the development of the factory system and mass production. People had to be legally free to move to where the work was, instead of being tied to the land. The landowners also had to be legally free to accumulate wealth and to be able to invest it to make a profit.

According to Marx, no social system has appeared accidentally, but when it was historically necessary. Each new system outlives its usefulness. Within every process, internal contradictions take place, which bring down the system. Nothing can remain stable as the social structure is dependent on the economic base. This is the basic premise of dialectical materialism.

Marx believed that the basic key to understanding the history of human society was exploitation. To Marx, class divisions were not simply between rich and poor. Classes were defined by how people stood in relation to the means of production. Those who produced food, clothing, shelter and so on have always been exploited. The surplus products they made were always controlled by a class of non-producers, except in very primitive societies. For example, in medieval, feudal societies everyone had to give a tenth of their produce (a tithe) to the Church.

To Marx, the history of the world was the history of class warfare. Classes must always be in competition with those that are above or below them. Because Marx believed in a dialectical structure to society, he saw it as a construction of opposites that would always be in conflict. He believed that classes only really existed because of their antagonism to each other, that they were defined by that antagonism and that people who lived in such a society could never live harmoniously together. He believed the course of history was economically determined and capitalism could only end in revolution.

Class in the capitalist society

In the *Communist Manifesto*, Marx described how capitalism had divided society into the two opposing camps: the proletariat and the bourgeoisie. 'Bourgeois' is a term that is often used today in an insulting way to describe someone with narrow-minded middle-class tastes, but Marx based his structure of class on economic factors alone and not those of taste or habit. The use of the word in English probably came from the French Revolution, for the bourgeois were originally the French middle class, a class of merchants and small businessmen who became more powerful after the nobility fell out of favour with the masses.

Marx used the words bourgeoisie and capitalist interchangeably to describe the class that derived income from ownership or trade in capital assets, or from buying and selling commodities or services. On the other hand, the proletariat, or workers, did not own the means of production and had to sell their labour to the capitalists in order to live. There is no other way for workers to survive under a capitalist system, for they rely on wages to buy their means of subsistence: food, clothing and shelter.

Marx did acknowledge that other classes existed, but he believed they were becoming increasingly a part of the two main classes and these were becoming more and more polarized as capitalism progressed.

* The self-employed or 'petty bourgeoisie' were usually those who had small family firms, owned some means of production and worked for themselves. The successful ones would rise to the ranks of the bourgeoisie, the rest would be pushed down into the proletariat.
* In Marx's day there was also a huge mass of domestic servants who had a better standard of living than many factory workers.

* Managerial workers, such as factory supervisors, are also wage labourers but they are slightly more privileged than ordinary workers.
* Peasants worked largely on the land without much use of machinery up until the twentieth century and they still represented a large part of the European population in the time of Marx. He acknowledged that they were a separate class, but did not think they would be easy to involve in any class struggle.
* There was also what Marx called the 'stagnant element', the 'lumpenproletariat', the large mass of unemployables who do not really fit into society at all: 'thieves, vagabonds ... the demoralized, the ragged'.

Marx recognized that these other classes did exist but he saw that under capitalism this class structure was becoming simpler and polarized into extremes. Marx saw that exploitation and oppression of the workers was the norm of the society but wondered why the proletariat wasn't doing anything about it. He believed the answer lay in the alienation of the workers and in something he called ideology.

Ideology

According to Marx, each society is unique and has its own ideology: each society has its own assumptions about the nature of humanity and has its own morality and values. At the time that Marx was writing, most philosophers believed ideas and consciousness were the shaping forces of world history. Marx's materialist view divided society into the 'economic base' and the 'superstructure'. He believed that the way people thought was a reflection of the economic base of the country that they lived in.

The economic base is really a combination of two things: 'productive forces', as Marx called them, and 'relations of production'.

Productive forces are material things used to produce commodities. These include things such as raw materials, machinery and the labour power of the workers who use them. For example, in a feudal society a weaver might use a hand loom to turn sheep's wool into cloth, so the wool, loom and the work he does with them are productive forces.

Relations of production are the relationships between people or between people and things. For example, the loom may belong to a family of weavers who use it to make cloth that they can sell to rich customers. The relationships in the family, and of the family to their customers, are relations of production. In a feudal society, the relationship between a serf and his lord, described earlier in this chapter, is one example of a relation of production.

Marx saw this economic base, formed by the productive forces and the relations of production, as intrinsic to the development of the superstructure of society.

The superstructure of society consists of its laws, culture, customs, religions and government. In a feudal society the economic base of society depended on its hierarchical structure. The loyalty of the serf to his lord was fundamental to the way society worked, so the superstructure of that society emphasized morality and religion, ideas of co-operation, obedience, and loyalty. This was entrenched in the morality of the Church and in the property laws. People 'belonged' to other people and to the land they worked on and they had a fixed place in the class hierarchy that was difficult to change; it was only in fairy stories that the goose girl got to marry the prince.

Marx believed that the economic base leads the development of the superstructure; the superstructure only exists in the form that it does because of the economic base. The productive forces changed radically during the Industrial Revolution. For example, small hand-looms were replaced by huge steam-driven ones in large factories, which needed hundreds of workers. It was no longer possible for society to function on a feudal basis; workers needed to be available on the free market and not tied to the land. The new relations of production were between boss and worker and so the political and legal superstructure had to change to accommodate the ideas of competitiveness and freedom of the individual.

Social consciousness, people's ideas, assumptions and ways of thinking reflected the society that they lived in, so society was shaped by the modes of production prevalent at that time. Marx believed the same economic base would sustain many different kinds of society, depending on historical and political factors. Even two fairly similar capitalist countries will have different social values. For example, although Britain, France and Germany are all capitalist countries in Europe they have very different cultures. Marx believed that the contradictions in the economic base were the driving force in historical struggle.

Marx believed that the ideas that rule any country, and the laws that develop from them, must be the ideas of the ruling class. These rules naturally develop from the society as it changes. They are not worked out in advance. When feudalism developed into capitalism, nobody sat down and worked out that they would need to have a population that was free to move around the country to find work instead of being tied to the land. It was just that the new necessities of life meant that society had to develop in the way that it did. People had to take risks and work out solutions to the new problems that the new economic structure posed. Because the way that people actually think is influenced by the society around them and the society that went before, people find it difficult to develop entirely new ideas. They can only think in the way that their language and the concepts handed down to them allow. When people cannot see the way their beliefs are artificially constructed by society it is known in Marxist terms as false consciousness.

Most people tend to believe that the world around them is in a finished, fixed form which cannot be changed. They do not examine the way in which the society around them came about or what processes it went through to get there. This makes it difficult for them to envisage any kind of change to the system. At the time Marx was writing, the divisions between the capitalist and the worker were seen as part of human nature and the natural order of society. This was reinforced by the fact that the capitalists control information, education, religion and entertainment.

Also, most working-class people were not considered worthy of education and were not eligible to vote during most of the time Marx was alive. This must have affected the aspirations of people, as they would have valued themselves as unworthy citizens.

Marx believed that the only way to counteract this kind of thinking was a revolutionary workers' party, which would educate the workers so that they understood the ways in which they were being exploited and help them to revolt against it. Today we are much more aware of the conditioning of society and media manipulation, but only because Marx brought attention to the problem over a hundred years ago.

Class struggle

In the nineteenth century everybody took the class structure for granted, as if it had always existed in its current form. Marx believed that classes had never existed in exactly that way before because the economic structure of society had not existed in a capitalist form before. He believed that class structure had become much simpler than it had been before and it was the needs of the capitalist system that had actually brought the working class into existence. The capitalist system needed wage labourers to survive, but in creating this class it had actually sown the seeds of its own destruction.

The aim of the bourgeoisie, or capitalist class, was to increase its profits by any means possible. The aim of the proletariat, or workers, was to improve its living and working conditions. Marx believed these needs were obviously in conflict and would lead to class struggle and ultimately to revolution. Class struggle does not necessarily mean violent struggle, although Marx did believe that this would occur. Class struggle can be any social action that results from the different interests of classes; for example, demonstrating or writing a letter of protest.

In Marxist theory it is seen as necessary to allow class consciousness to develop. Marx talked of a class 'in itself' and a class 'for itself'.

* A class 'in itself' refers to a group of individuals who share the same relationship to the means of production and share common interests.
* A class 'for itself' is a class that is conscious of these interests; a class that has discovered that it is alienated.

The way for workers to realize they are alienated is through education and by political means. Marx thought that the workers were in a unique position within the capitalist system as they were the only class capable of bringing about a revolution. They were the only class in society who could achieve a new form of society, a communist society.

Workers' power and education

Although the dialectical view of history states that capitalism will eventually bring about its own downfall, Marx did not think that it would happen automatically without anyone having to do anything. Although he was a great philosopher, he did not just talk idly of class struggle, he was also actively involved in the workers' movement, especially in his early life. Exiled in Paris he met with workers and was impressed by their character and strength; this led to his involvement with the League of the Just and the Communist League.

There were very few properly organized workers' groups in London when Marx moved there. Many of them had to be very secretive for fear of reprisals; anyone seen to be causing problems within the workplace was likely to be dismissed at the very least. But there were some movements towards change in society that had large elements of worker involvement, such as:
* the Chartists
* trade unions
* the Communist League
* the International Workingmen's Association.

Marx was ahead of his time in understanding the importance of modern technology and communications to the revolutionary cause.

Contact among groups could be made and eventually the numerous local struggles could be centralized to become a national struggle between the classes. Eventually, an international struggle would take place.

Is revolution inevitable?

Marx developed his views on revolution throughout his lifetime but on the whole he was in favour of revolution, although he did not believe it would necessarily have to be violent. At the conference of the International he addressed these words to the government, 'we will proceed against you by peaceful means where it is possible and with arms when it is necessary'.

The conclusion he drew from his dialectical study of society was that revolution was not only desirable but also inevitable because of the internal conflicts inherent in capitalism. According to Marx, these polar opposites could not exist together in a stable society; dialectical theory would mean that the proletariat must overthrow the bourgeoisie.

He believed that a better society could then be built, a society based on the principles of communism. A communist society would not be able to be built straight after a revolution, but would develop over time, after initial stages of socialism.

Marx was not the first to believe that society should be improved; many of his ideas were developed from those of the Utopian Socialists. Where Marx differed from them was in the choice of method that would bring about this society. The Utopians believed reason was the best way to bring about a change in the views of society. They set up model communities and factories where hours were regulated; workers were treated fairly and given access to education, good homes and nourishing food. They believed these examples of philanthropy would be enough to bring about change in society.

Marx agreed with the humanitarian changes which were made, but thought that good housing, medical care, education and wage reforms did not get to the root of the problem, which was the exploitation of one class by another. If the economic base of society is the real source of the conflicts within it, no amount of workers' benefits will resolve the problem. The contradictions within the capitalist system will continue to accumulate. Change will only come about when workers take over factories, mines and banks by force. Another reason why Marx believed in the inevitability of revolution was his view of the state. He was the first to realize that 'the state' is not an impartial body that works for the benefit of everybody in society. He believed the state exists to protect the ruling class and suppress those that produce wealth for them. These factors make it even more likely that revolution must take place against the vested interests in capitalism. The state will try to block any peaceful or non-confrontational changes that undermine its powers of suppression.

In his early years, Marx believed that revolution would:

* begin in the industrialized capitalist countries of Europe such as Britain and Prussia
* spread rapidly around the rest of the world because of the way in which countries had become economically dependent on each other.

Marx was disappointed that in his lifetime the predicted revolution did not occur, despite a number of simultaneous strikes and uprisings that happened throughout Europe in 1848. He and Engels became very excited by the bourgeois revolution in Germany that year and predicted it would soon spread, but when this did not materialize he wondered if perhaps the time was not quite right. In later years he predicted that workers might have to go through at least 50 years of struggle before they could change their circumstances, and that this would be a long-term process.

Marx was always against revolutionary terror of the kind that had happened in France and thought it showed immaturity on the part of the participants. For this reason, he was against revolution taking place too soon, when people were not educated enough to take part properly in the process of change.

6

further Marxist thought

Although Marx wrote a great deal about the way in which the relationship between society and the economy had developed throughout history, he did not write much about how these would develop after the revolution that he had predicted. He believed a classless communist society would be the result of the revolution, but he did not really define how this society might be run. He made a few predictions about what might happen and some of these were influenced by the ideas of the Utopian Socialists, although he did not agree with a lot of their more Romantic ideals.

Although he did not write in detail about the structure of any future communist society, he thought deeply about the relationships between people within that society. In his writing he looked at the world in a new way and shed new light on the relationships between individuals and the society they lived in. His ideas were considered extremely radical in their day but today we take many of them for granted in Western society; for example, equal rights for men, women and children.

After the revolution

Marx did not write a great deal about the form that society would take after the revolution, or how it would be organized. He believed that society would have to become a communist one in the long term, but there would have to be a transitional phase before this could occur, there would have to be an intermediate stage known as socialism. Socialism in the Marxist sense is just a descriptive word for the intermediate stage between capitalism and communism. Today the word socialism has become a much less easily defined term, referring to any system where there is state control, planning and ownership of the means of production. There is also some element of social care for the sick, children, the elderly and those in extreme poverty.

Communist society

Marx believed that once the proletariat had achieved state power they could take control of the means of production. Eventually class distinctions would be abolished and a classless communist society would be the result. Society would not be based on one class exploiting another class; workers would be in control of the means of production and they would use the wealth produced for the good of society as a whole. Society would be a self-governing community.

Marx believed society would eventually be stateless because he believed the state was a tool that let one branch of society oppress another. He felt that when classes were finally abolished then 'the power of the state, whose function is to keep the great majority of producers beneath the yoke of a small minority of exploiters, will disappear and government functions will be transformed into simple administrative functions'.

After the revolution, the state would 'wither away' as there would be no oppression, but it would take time. Engels said that 'the proletariat seizes political power and turns the means of production in the first instance into state property. But in doing this it abolishes itself as the proletariat'. In order to do this, society would need to be more productive with a much shorter working day so that people would have time to participate in running the society.

Because he believed the ownership of property defines the class system, it was important to Marx that private property should be abolished. This would mean that classes would eventually cease to exist, so there would be no inequality and no need for further class struggle. He also thought that when the means of production were centralized, private property would disappear and money would then cease to exist.

Marx and Engels firmly believed that the revolution would be an international one. This would mean that the army would have a purely internal peacekeeping function and money would not need to be spent on defence.

The main writings we have on the form that a communist society would take are *The Principles of Communism*, written by Engels in 1847. These set out the views of the Communist League, of which Marx was a member. These are the main points of the document:

* Limitation of private property through progressive taxation, inheritance tax and abolition of inheritance rights for the family.
* Capitalists to be expropriated through competition with state industry and partial compensation.
* Confiscation of the possessions of emigrants and rebels against the majority.
* Central organization of wages for workers on the land or in factories. Competition between workers to be abolished.
* All members of society to be equally liable for work until private property is abolished. Industrial armies to be formed, especially for agriculture.
* Private banks to be suppressed and money and credit to be centralized in national banks.
* State-owned factories, workshops, etc. to be developed as far as economically feasible; agriculture to be improved.
* Education for all children at schools paid for by the State.
* Communal dwellings to be built on waste land to combine the best of rural and urban life.

* Unhygienic, badly built slum housing to be destroyed.
* Equal inheritance rights for children born out of wedlock.
* Transport to be nationalized.

It was not considered feasible that all these changes could take place at once. It was felt that once one change was made others would follow and they would accumulate. The abolition of private property would be the first step and then agriculture, transport and trade would be centralized.

Marx and Engels didn't consider the future communist society to be a utopian one or that it was based on utopian principles. They wrote in the *Communist Manifesto*, 'the theoretical conclusions of the communists are in no way based on the ideas or principles that have been invented, or discovered by this or that would-be universal reformer'. Engels was a great admirer of Fourier though, as can be seen in his idea of building communal dwellings combining urban and rural living.

Marx did not want a return to some idealized rural society; he saw that technological progress was one of the main benefits that capitalism had brought to society and he believed that development of this would lead to huge improvements in society. It would allow for more leisure time and time for education, and would help society to become stateless because the working week would be shorter and everyone would be able to participate in running society. It would also lead to material abundance for all.

Surplus labour would still exist but it would not be hidden by any kind of exploitation or fetishism. In the third volume of *Das Kapital*, Marx had the idea that these surpluses would be used in a kind of welfare state. Everyone who could work would have to work, but the surplus product would be set aside and divided between those who could not support themselves; those who 'on account of age are not yet, or no longer able to take part in production'. He did not believe that anyone else should be supported by the state though, for he also wrote that, 'all labour to support those who do not work would cease'.

Communist society would be a hardworking and productive place, but both Marx and Engels hoped that work in a communist society would be enjoyable and not an oppressive means of survival. It was hoped that after the initial stages of communism, where people were still attached to old capitalist ways of thinking, then a communist society would take into account people's varying needs and abilities. Marx wrote in the *Gotha Programme*:

'In a higher phase of communist society, after the enslaving subordination of the individual to the division of labour, and therewith also the antithesis between mental and physical labour, has vanished; after labour has become not only a means of life but life's prime want; after the productive forces have also increased with all-round development of the individual, and all the springs of co-operative wealth flow more abundantly – only then can the narrow horizon of bourgeois right be crossed in its entirety and society inscribe on its banners: From each according to his ability, to each according to his needs!'

Religion

'Religion is the opium of the people', is one of Marx's most famous quotations. Opium is an addictive drug that dulls the senses, and Marx believed that religion had a similar effect in capitalist society. He had seen some of the problems that religion caused for his own family when his father renounced his Jewish faith. Prussia was an anti-Semitic country and Jews were not allowed to hold public office. He saw that religion was a part of the state system that could be used as a form of oppression and as a part of the false consciousness that added to the alienation of the populace.

Marx himself was an atheist and was greatly influenced by materialist philosophers and free thinkers such as Hume and Diderot, who had concentrated on finding rational arguments against religion. Being believers in scientific order and rationalism, they thought they could prove by scientific means that God could not exist. They thought that most people had a superstitious belief in God that would disappear when they were enlightened by the powers of reason.

Marx agreed with these rationalist philosophers to some extent, but his views on alienation meant that he believed a purely rationalist view of the world was not enough to change it.

He was greatly influenced by Feuerbach who said the essence
of Christianity was the essence of mankind itself. Marx believed
that God was created by human consciousness and was a product
of human minds, but he wanted to understand why people
worshipped God and why their religious beliefs took the form that
they did. Eventually, he came to the conclusion that religion is part
of the ideological make-up of society:

* In primitive societies, where people's lives are dependent
  on their relationship with the natural world, religion helps
  to unite them with nature. Natural forces are worshipped
  as gods and the natural cycles of their world become part
  of the religion.
* In more developed societies, people become freed from
  their dependence on nature by use of technology but they
  feel alienated from society because they have little control
  over their daily lives. People then use religion as a means of
  expressing their frustrations.

Marx believed that any fulfilment people gained from religion
was illusory because religion is just another form of alienation.
People do not realize they are not free and, until they do, they cannot
change society so there is little to be achieved by demonstrating
a lack of science and reason in religion. In this way he differed from
the philosophers who came before him – Hegel, Feuerbach and
the other Young Hegelians. They believed the alienation people felt
was because they did not understand the progress of the universal
mind and once they saw their place in this, through philosophical
enlightenment, they would see things clearly, as they truly are,
and without any religious false consciousness. Their lives would
then have meaning.

Marx believed that people felt that their lives were
meaningless because they were actually meaningless. Capitalism
is a social system that means we are unfulfilled as human beings.
'Religious distress is at the same time the expression of real distress
and also the protest against real distress. Religion is the sigh of the
oppressed creature, the heart of a heartless world, just as it is the
spirit of spiritless conditions. It is the opium of the people.'

Marx could see that religion served a very important function in capitalist society. Religion acknowledges the alienation of the individual but says this is because they are separated from God. This is useful, for it stops people questioning whether their feelings are due to the way their society is structured. They feel that alienation is a part of the natural condition of humanity.

Religion leads people to believe that there is a purpose to their suffering which they might not understand but gives promises of an afterlife if they follow certain spiritual practices. It exaggerates the alienation of the individual and offers them a long-term cure at the same time. It also brings reassurance, for many people need their religious illusions as a prop and as a comfort in a harsh environment.

Marx saw that merely understanding the problem was not enough; philosophy itself cannot change the world. Understanding why you feel alienated is only the beginning. Religion will only cease to exist when alienation ceases to exist and this cannot happen until certain classes are no longer oppressed and everybody becomes equal in a communist society: 'The abolition of religion, as the illusory happiness of men, is a demand for their real happiness. The call to abandon their illusions about their condition is a call to abandon a condition which requires illusions.'

Women's rights and the family

In the *Communist Manifesto*, Marx and Engels take great pains to point out that the communists are not about to introduce 'a community of women' and break up the family. They had been accused of this in the press several times that year. At that time, few women in capitalist countries had the vote, and in the eyes of the law they were seen as possessions belonging to their husbands. A community of women implied women who would be free to give their sexual favours to anyone they chose. Marx pointed out in the *Communist Manifesto* that the bourgeoisie used their wives like instruments of production and feared that, as instruments of production were to be exploited, then the same fate would happen to their wives. He argued that marriage could be considered as a legalized form of prostitution, and he concluded that only through the abolition of the class system would prostitution, 'both public and private', be abolished.

Much of Marxist thought on women and the family arises from the work of Engels. There are no other communist writers of that time who wrote on the rights of women as being separate from the rights of workers as a whole class. In 1845 Engels wrote *The Origin of the Family, Private Property and the State*. In this, he argues that monogamous marriage is a social institution that exists in relation to private property and that women must be economically independent from men before they can be truly emancipated. One of the best-known quotations from this work is: 'The modern individual family is based on the open or disguised enslavement of the woman.'

Marx wanted everybody to be equal – men, women and children – and he believed that a communist society without private property would ensure this. He felt that relations between the sexes and relations between parents and children were corrupted by wage labour and private property. In the *Communist Manifesto* he wrote: 'All family ties between the proletariat are torn asunder, children transformed into simple articles of commerce and instruments of labour.'

Class divisions at that time meant that men, women and children from the working class laboured for long hours in factories and mines. They had few opportunities for health care or education. Women in the middle classes did not work outside the home after marriage and it was not always seen as necessary to educate girls. Marx believed that marriage could never be an equal partnership when women were treated as second-class citizens and men were seen as the head of the household, for this stopped women from reaching their true potential as individuals.

In an ideal communist society, Marx believed there would be equal access for all to work and education. Adequate childcare facilities would mean that women would no longer have to be financially dependent on their husbands. Women would not be financially disadvantaged by bearing children and caring for them. Marx believed that bringing all women into the workplace was the first step towards giving them equality. It would be the first step in getting them involved in planning the economy, and so changing society. It would also be the first step in abolishing prostitution, which he saw as a by-product of the capitalist system that viewed everything in financial terms.

Marx always thought that it was not enough just to pass liberal laws giving rights to minorities if the whole structure of society and the economy remains the same. Laws can be passed to give rights to women, but it is only when the ideology of the society changes, so that women do not bear the entire burden of care of the young and elderly, that women will be emancipated. This proved to be correct in many so-called communist societies where women did a day's work, often in physically demanding jobs, but found that it was still their job to do the housework and the shopping. Modern capitalist society is quite often the same.

Feminism grew rapidly in the twentieth century from small beginnings in the nineteenth century, and although many modern-day feminists would disagree with the views of Marx and Engels and their analysis of the place of women, it cannot be denied that they were some of the earliest social reformers to look at the position of women in society in a systematic way. Marxist feminism is still an important part of the whole feminist movement and the emphasis of Marxist feminists is mainly on the belief that capitalism is the root of women's oppression and that women's subordination is really a form of class oppression. A lot of their work is centred around the workplace; examining why women still have low wages and the ways in which women's domestic work is trivialized by capitalism. Many of them admire the way Marx exposed how social, economic and political structures can cause alienation.

Art and culture

Marx believed art and culture was an important part of any society. He believed an appreciation of this is vital for everybody in the society, for it helps us to understand that society and also ourselves. He was very fond of using quotations from Greek literature and Shakespeare in his work; *Das Kapital* is full of such references. This made it difficult for ordinary working people to understand; most preferred to read Engels, who wrote in a more straightforward manner. Of course, many workers at that time could not read at all because they were not educated. This illustrates Marx's first point:

* Art is mainly for the minority. In a capitalist system, it is selected by a minority. Their freedom to enjoy art is at the expense of those who work to produce the wealth that gives them the money and leisure time to enjoy art. Artists have to supply art that will satisfy the requirements and taste of this minority. This leads to his second point.

* Capitalist society tends to see everything in financial terms. Everything is given a financial 'value'. Freedom of expression, craftsmanship and making things for their own sake become subordinated by time and money.

Marx believed that art, like society, developed as a series of dialectical contradictions.

As members of a society, artists, writers and musicians must also be influenced by the prevailing ideology. There will always be a few who struggle to express themselves in new ways, contradicting the old forms of artistic expression. In this way, art can subvert the bourgeois prejudices that prevail in a capitalist society.

Marx believed that in the ideal communist society everyone will have access to the cultural heritage of society and artistic activities will stop being the preserve of a privileged minority.

Freedom and the individual

Marx saw individuals as products of the society to which they belong. Each society has its own view on individuality because each society has its own ideology. Every different social system will place a different emphasis on the relationship between the individual and society. In certain societies, for example capitalist ones, the rights of the individual are highly prized. In other societies the rights of the group are seen as more important than the rights of the individual.

Marx wrote of the alienation in the capitalist system, which led to competitive struggle between individuals. He felt this was a necessary stage on the way to communism, where people would find their true individuality without the need for destructive competitiveness. Because Marx believed it was the capitalist work system that stopped the individual reaching his true potential, he felt only the rise of the proletariat and the change to a communist society would allow the individual his full rights. In the proposed communist society:

* labour would be planned for producing the means of life, according to agreed needs
* labour time would be reduced to increase free time for everyone. This would lead to artistic and scientific development for all and would lead to greater self-knowledge.

Marx did not think that greed and envy were intrinsic to human nature, and stated that if private property and capitalist ways of working were changed to a system of communal property and a communal means of production, then people would no longer be in competition with each other. There would be no false consciousness and no exploitation. At the time Marx was writing, workers' groups were fighting for the essential rights of freedom:

* freedom of speech
* freedom of assembly
* freedom of the press
* equality under the law
* equal rights to vote.

Marx did not disagree with any of these rights, but he believed that as long as the economic base of society was still capitalist then people were not free, even if they had the rights by law. For example, although in the eyes of the law everybody is equal, those who are better off can afford better representation in court; there may be freedom of the press but only the very rich can afford to own a major newspaper. It is only when capitalism is overthrown by revolution that true freedom will occur.

Marxism
after Marx

Karl Marx died in 1883 but his work carried on. As his ideas began to be spread around the world they lead to changes in political systems that still affect the world we live in today. Because of the vast body of his work and its complexity, it is easy for people to interpret his ideas in their own way and claim that their interpretation is the 'true' meaning of Marxism. As Marx did not write much about how communism would work, many widely differing types of communism emerged. Many different regimes have called themselves Marxist or communist, but they did not necessarily have similar ideologies or political systems. In fact, they may well have very little in common with the original ideas of Marx, except for the use of his name. Marx became so upset by the many misinterpretations of his ideas that he is reported to have said: 'All I know is that I am not a Marxist.'

In this chapter we will look at some of the ways that his ideas were interpreted, leading to revolution and world change, and examine if they are still relevant in the twenty-first century.

The spread of Marxist thought

Karl Marx died in 1883 but his work carried on. Engels considered himself to be a 'mere talent' compared to the genius of Marx; he wrote to an old friend, F. A. Sorge, after Marx's death, 'the proletarian movement will go on, but the centre is gone'. Engels then had to become that centre. He shared some of the work with Marx's youngest daughter Eleanor (Tussy). Although Engels edited and published the later volumes of *Das Kapital*, it was Eleanor who did a lot of the background work: researching, checking and annotating references. She also did a lot of translation work. Volume 2 of *Das Kapital* was first published in Germany in 1885 and Volume 3 was published in 1894. Although the first English translation sold badly, the second edition, brought out in 1895, sold out in a few months; the philosophy of communism that Marx and Engels had developed together began to spread around the world, mainly through the labour movement and working men's groups.

Engels became a popular figure among the new Marxist groups that began springing up as a result of the translations of Marx's works; he gave advice to labour movements and to those who were beginning to organize the new International Workingmen's Association. He wrote articles in German, Austrian and French publications and became involved with working-men's associations throughout Europe, including Spain, Denmark, Bulgaria and Serbia.

The international labour movement was growing rapidly, and it was through this that the ideas of Marx began to take hold on the minds of workers throughout the world. Marx's ideas became the basis of many socialist parties throughout Europe, although many of them did not advocate revolution, preferring to change society by means of reform. Marx's analysis of the capitalist system and the way in which it exploited workers gave them a base on which to structure their justification for reform. From the widely differing versions of communism that developed after Marx's death there emerged two main strands:

* **Evolutionary communism** – Evolutionary communists believe in the power of the evolution of society.

Communism will come about through the natural progress of society and the disintegration of the capitalist system, due to its internal flaws. Evolutionary communists resemble Socialist Utopians to some extent in their belief that society can be changed for the better without revolution. These 'reformists' want to work within existing political systems.

* **Revolutionary communism** – Revolutionary communists believe the power of revolution is the only way to change society. Communism will come about only through the overthrow of the bourgeoisie by violent means, including terrorism. Terrorists do not necessarily believe the State can be defeated by their actions but hope to destroy the morale of the people and their support for the government.

As Engels travelled though Europe speaking to workers' groups, the crowds coming to listen became larger and larger and he began to get standing ovations. In the fourth German edition of the *Communist Manifesto*, he expressed a deep regret that Marx could not see how much the international labour movement was growing. He died in August 1895 of cancer of the oesophagus; he was cremated and his ashes were scattered off Beachy Head on the south coast of England.

Eleanor Marx was a popular speaker on socialist topics and on women's rights. She led mass rallies on the shorter working day in Hyde Park and played an active part in organizing strikes among women who worked in match factories. Sadly, her work in disseminating her father's ideas was cut short as she committed suicide in 1898; it was thought this was due to problems in her relationship with Edward Aveling.

The development of socialism

The socialist and communist movements in Europe at the end of the nineteenth century were closely intertwined. At first, they both mainly concentrated on workers' rights and on universal suffrage. Both movements were based on the theories of Marx, but it became apparent as time went on that some people were more moderate than others and a split began between the followers of evolutionary and revolutionary strands of thought. Socialism is a word that can be confusing in Marxist literature because the term in general use differs from the Marxist term. Generally it is taken to indicate belief in a socio-economic system with some kind of State or collective ownership of the means of production, but it is a very vague term that covers many diverse types of government. In the main, it differs from communism because this is usually identified with a one-party totalitarian state. In classical Marxism, Marx is often described as a 'scientific socialist' and socialism refers to the period occurring just after the revolution before true communism is reached. This is how confusion often occurs.

Russian communism

Russia was the first communist country in the world. The type of communism that eventually evolved there had little in common with Marx's ideals but because it was the first communist country, and the only communist country for many years, people often believe that Russian communism is 'true communism'.

The first revolutionary communists were the Russian Bolsheviks, led by Lenin. They overthrew the Romanov dynasty that had ruled the country in a feudal manner for 300 years. The communist uprising of 1917 came as a surprise to most of the world, which had never heard of communism or Karl Marx.

Marxism came to Russia through the work of Georgi Plekhanov, son of a landowner. His ideas were carried by students to factories and towns and one of his chief converts was Vladimir Ilyich Ulyanov, later to be known as Lenin. Lenin became a ruthless leader of the people and took advantage of the chaos in his country to take power. Although Lenin was a charismatic leader, it was not just his interpretation of Marx that led to revolution. It was a war that Marx could not have foreseen that became the catalyst for revolution and led to the first communist state.

Russia was already ravaged by industrial unrest and social dissatisfaction when the First World War began. Initial patriotism turned into discontent, especially as many lives and areas of land were lost. Refugees caused a housing crisis, people were starving and prices were rising. The population became demoralized and war-weary. Lenin realized that peace was important to the population and insisted that the war would only end if capitalism was overthrown. He called for the peasants to re-distribute the land and for political power to be held by the soviets, a kind of local council. (This is why Russia became known later as the Soviet Union or USSR). The Bolsheviks took power in October 1917 and declared a decree on peace. Lenin inaugurated the dictatorship of the proletariat to justify the role of the Communist Party, which did not have the complete support of the population.

After many years of civil war in Russia, a so-called communist state eventually evolved which had very little to do with the society envisaged by Marx and Engels. At first, things looked favourable: free enterprise was abolished; land, banks, foreign trade and shipping were nationalized. These measures should have been the start of the ideal communist state that Marx believed in. However, Russia was really not developed enough economically for true communism to exist. The civil war that ravaged Russia after the revolution left the economy in ruins and the idealist leaders of the first revolution were eventually replaced or died, some in suspicious circumstances. Joseph Stalin became the virtual dictator after Lenin's death and the state that should have 'withered away' became all-powerful. Stalin had to make Russia economically viable; to this end, he pushed through several disastrous policies, which were intended to bring the very backward peasant economy in line with the major capitalist nations. The Soviet Union was ostensibly a Marxist-Leninist regime under his rule but this was nothing like the society envisaged by either Marx or Lenin.

After Stalin

Stalin ran the Soviet Union as a totalitarian state, and after his death in 1953 the leader who followed him, Nikita Khrushchev, denounced him as a dictator. Khrushchev wished to go back to the ideals of Marx and Lenin and this heightened differences with the regime in communist China (which until then had been one of its main allies), leading to a split between the two countries. The Soviet Union became even more isolated economically from the rest of the world and also politically as the Cold War began to take hold. Eventually it was broken up in 1991.

Chinese communism

Russia remained the only communist country in the world until joined by China, which had a largely rural and illiterate population and little industrialization. It was ruled over by a warlord class in a feudal manner. After many years of fighting, the People's Liberation Army, under the leadership of Chairman Mao, declared the People's Republic of China in 1949. Mao was a brilliant military strategist and expert in guerrilla warfare. His victory, much like that of the Bolsheviks in Russia, was aided by another war that affected the internal conflict. When Japanese forces invaded China, in the Sino-Japanese war of 1937, many people joined with the communists in order to flee from the Japanese.

Chairman Mao wanted to educate the peasants into the ways of communism, so he wrote many texts loosely based on those of Marx. These became the basis of Chinese communism, also called Maoism or Mao Zedong thought, and were eventually published in the West as the infamous 'little red book'. This was sold very cheaply around the world during the 1960s.

Maoism is a further development of Marxist thought, and although it is officially still a part of Chinese communism in the twenty-first century, its influence has been greatly reduced since the death of Chairman Mao in 1976. Maoist thought differed from the traditional Marxist-Leninist policies and was much more militaristic. Mao stressed the importance of changing the whole mental outlook of society by transforming education, literature, art and any other parts of the superstructure that did not correspond to the socialist economic base. It was felt that the only true communists were the proletariat and anybody else was likely to be an 'imperialist'.

The Red Guard, composed mainly of students, was an all-powerful communist militia that imposed communist thought on the populace. Anyone considered to be an 'imperialist' was purged; intellectuals and anyone believed to have bourgeois thoughts were imprisoned, exiled to work in labour camps or re-educated; many disappeared. Traditional Chinese culture was ignored and followers of all religions were persecuted.

Since Mao's death, China has been gradually moving towards a free market economy and has seen a huge increase in economic growth since the 1990s. China is still officially a communist state under an authoritarian single party system, but many would say it is communist in name only.

The Cold War

'A spectre is haunting Europe, the spectre of communism', wrote Marx in the *Communist Manifesto*. After the Second World War the spectre of communism seemed to be haunting the whole world. This was the period of the Cold War when it seemed everyone was on the alert for 'reds under the bed'. The Cold War did not result in an actual military war with open hostility; it was a prolonged series of political, ideological and economic conflicts between communist and capitalist countries that lasted for about 45 years. It centred round a huge arms race involving nuclear and conventional weapons, largely between the superpowers of the USA and the USSR. It was feared that this would lead to a full-blown conflict, perhaps involving nuclear weapons, in which millions of people would be killed and the world totally destroyed.

In addition to the arms race, there was a huge propaganda war involving espionage and spy scandals and a kind of economic war with blockades and trade embargoes. Also, what have been called 'proxy wars' took place, where the superpowers became embroiled in the internal policies of overseas nations during civil wars, such as in Korea and Vietnam.

There were three main factors that led to the Cold War.

* Europe had been divided by peace treaty after the Second World War and many European countries came under communist control as part of the Soviet bloc.

The Soviet Union was now one of the major powers and it influenced governments in countries around it using military and economic aid. Berlin became divided by the Berlin Wall. An 'Iron Curtain' of secrecy was said to have come down between Eastern and Western Europe.

* There were fears that Communist China would come to dominate South East Asia. It was felt that 'the loss of Indo-China will cause the fall of South East Asia like a set of dominoes'. This was the domino theory, as described by President Eisenhower, and it led to the United States' involvement in Laos, Cambodia, Korea and, ultimately, to the Vietnam War.
* There were revolutions in South America and Africa against colonial oppression. Many of the countries involved received aid from the Communist bloc in their struggle for independence.

Whatever the reasons for its origin, the Cold War was largely an ideological war based on fear and mistrust that came from deep differences between the communist and capitalist blocs. It came to an end in the 1980s, largely due to the decline of the communist economy in the Soviet Union and the People's Republic of China.

Has Marxism failed?

Was the decline of the Soviet Union the beginning of the end for Marxism? Many people would argue that this is the case, but the response of many Marxists would be to say that the regime in the Soviet Union had very little to do with Marx except for the use of his name. They would describe it as a form of state capitalism, where bureaucrats acted as a form of bourgeoisie. The fall of the Soviet Union led to a great crisis of confidence in other communist countries that saw the Soviet government as a model for them to follow. They also lost trade markets and military support.

Critics would also point to the fact that China is now largely a free market economy and not actually a communist state at all, and that the communist governments in Indo-China and in Cuba are reliant on Chinese economic support and so strictly speaking they cannot be described as communist either. Although officially North Korea (The Democratic People's Republic of Korea) is a socialist republic, it has been described as a dictatorship by its critics. There is some debate about the future of communism in Cuba after Fidel Castro's leadership ended. His age and ill health meant he passed the reins of government over to his younger brother in 2008. As personality cults are important in all communist states that developed out of peasant economies this change in leadership might affect the popularity of the communist government. There is much speculation as to how communism might develop in Cuba in the future.

Although it looks like the end for communism in many places, it has not stopped Marxists who are working towards power in the developing world, notably in India and Nepal. It is impossible to say what might happen in the future.

The development of Marxist thought

There is no doubt that the ideas of Marx changed the world. Revolutions happened in his name and communist societies came into being. His ideas also led to a great deal of debate about the nature of society and of humankind, for he changed the way that we look at each other and at the world. In academic circles there has been continuing debate and discussion of his ideas for over a century. This has led to the splitting off of different schools of thought based on Marxist ideas, but developing them further. Since the fall of the Soviet Union, there has been less interest in his work academically; it has become 'unfashionable', especially as the academic world moves towards postmodern theory. However, with the rise of anti-capitalist and anti-globalization campaigns, including the eco-socialist movement, there are signs that there may be future developments in the aspects of Marx's work that look at the 'destructive' spread of capitalism and its relation to ecology.

What follows aims to give some background understanding and structure to the many complex and conflicting theories that have been developed from the works of Marx. Some of these have been in favour academically and then gone out of favour again and some have always been controversial. However, it is important to have at least a basic understanding of them as many books on Marx assume knowledge of them.

There have also been numerous criticisms of his theories, especially as time has gone on. Many of his predictions do not seem to have come about and these will be discussed later.

Types of Marxism

Marx wrote a great deal and a great deal has been written about him, so that if someone claims to be a Marxist, the next question asked is often 'What kind?' As there have been numerous debates over who is the most accurate interpreter of what Marx wrote and many academic schools of Marxism exist, then this is not an easy question to answer. There is also some confusion over the word Marxian. Marxian is often used by those academics who agree with a lot of Marx's methodology but not in the conclusions he reached, or in his predictions about the future of society. It is often used in relation to the study of political and economic systems. For example, Marxian economics embraces Marx's use of the terms mode of production, surplus value, etc. However, those who use it do not necessarily believe the conclusions that Marx came to about alienation, exploitation and the need for revolution.

The main types of Marxism and schools of thought developed in response to his work are as follows:

* Classical Marxim
* Structural Marxism
* Gramsci's economic determinism
* Cultural Marxism (The Frankfurt School)
* The Praxis School (humanist)
* Analytical Marxism.

Post-Marxism

Post-Marxism is a term used to describe those who have built theories on those of Marx but have gone further, so that they are outside or beyond what was considered to be Marxist thought. Post-Marxists have moved away from the economic determinism that is implicit in Marx's work and disagree with his concept of class, but they do believe that there should be solidarity between members of society. **Ernesto Laclau** (1935–) and **Chantal Mouffe** (1943–) became the best known of the post-Marxists after the publication of their book *Hegemony and Socialist Strategy: Towards a Radical Democratic Politics* in 1985. In this they analysed classical Marxism but from a postmodern perspective, drawing on theories of language and deconstruction from Jacques Derrida and also exploring Antonio Gramsci's theory of hegemony, an extension of the theory of ideology. They believe that social conflicts arise out of 'antagonisms' within the hegemony that are difficult to understand because of the complexity of society and the personality. Postmodern thought sees the individual as a series of narratives; for example, Laclau and Mouffe saw that a working-class person is never just a 'working-class' person. They may be a single parent, from an ethnic minority, a woman and working class all at the same time. Each of these different facets of the personality may be in antagonism, or conflict, according to Laclau and Mouffe. Class is not a unifying structure at all. Everybody has a subjective view of society that depends on their experience; class identity is only a small part of this, so a class-based revolution is bound to fail. Conflicts will always be a part of society and it will always be unstable and changeable but people can group together, despite antagonisms, to take action at a local level.

Post-Marxists believe that the conventional democratic process actually alienates many people and they also believe that the state is always open to corruption, even under communism. They see a form of 'civil society' as the way forward, where people promote their own interests in the marketplace and achieve change by grouping together for local struggle.

Is Marxism relevant in the twenty-first century?

The beginning of the twentieth century saw a rise in world communism but by the end of the century it was in decline. At its peak, in the early 1980s, it was estimated that a third of the world lived under some kind of communist government but currently there are only a few communist regimes under a single party system: The People's Republic of China, Cuba, Laos, North Korea and Vietnam.

Many people see the collapse of communism as proof that Marx is not relevant to the world today. After the Soviet Union collapsed and the Berlin Wall came down, Communist China became more open to Western influence and its economy is now more open to free enterprise. People see the failure of communism as the failure of Marx, yet the communism that Marx envisaged has never existed. What the history of the twentieth century shows us is the power of Marx's ideas to capture the imaginations of the poor and oppressed throughout the world. There is no doubt that his beliefs, or others interpretations of them, changed the history of the world.

The relevance of Marx to today's society has been debated and discussed by many philosophers, economists, historians and other academics, as well as by fervent Marxists, students and drunken pub philosophers. Almost everyone has an opinion on Marx, even if it is not a particularly informed one. There are three main arguments:

1 Marxism is not relevant today at all because it was never relevant. His scientific method was flawed and his economic theory was completely mistaken.

2 Marxism is not relevant today because it was a product of its time. The capitalist society that existed at the time he was writing does not exist any more. There is no such thing as the proletariat now, so there will be no revolution. We are living in a postmodern world, which bears no resemblance to the nineteenth century. There is no such thing as class; huge theories of everything are false.

3 Marxism is still relevant. The failure of communism in some countries does not indicate that Marx was wrong. In fact he predicted there would be a swing away from his theories and that capitalism would try to fight back before it was finally defeated. The world may have changed but while the economy is a capitalist one, his theories are still relevant. Postmodern culture is an attempt to make people passive, interested in celebrity but unable to analyse anything.

The first theory is obviously wrong because even if Marx was totally mistaken about everything, many people have acted upon what he said, so it must have some relevance. The second and third theories can both be seen to be correct, to some extent, because of the sheer volume of work that Marx produced; it depends on which aspects of his work are being examined.

History

His 'scientific method' of studying history has been accused as not being scientific by modern standards. Karl Popper, a twentieth-century philosopher, believes that there is no real way of proving whether Marx's assertions are true or false as you could in a proper scientific study. However, Marx did amass and classify a great deal of evidence about past societies, and modern social science developed out of his techniques. He wrote and researched in a very structured way that attempted to use the scientific methods of his time, which were concerned with the classification of things.

Economy

Marx was not a trained economist. Some of his predictions about the economy have proved to be false; for example, wages being pushed down to subsistence level. On the contrary, most people are better off in real terms than they were a hundred years ago. Other assertions have been correct. He predicted that large corporations would come to dominate world markets. At the end of the twentieth century, more and more companies merged into large conglomerates. In the twenty-first century the trend continues with large supermarket chains taking each other over, buying up properties and forcing small shops out of business. Marx also predicted that industry would become more and more reliant on technology and that there would be periodic recessions – both of these predictions are correct. The latest recession, that began in 2007, happened on a global scale and was partly attributed to vast banking corporations.

Class and society

Society has changed for the better; in the Western World many inequalities have disappeared. Universal suffrage has changed the structure of society since Marx's time. In Britain we have free education up to university level and health services for all who need them, although many would see this as a two-tier system where the rich can afford to pay for better private treatment and education. However, it is still a great improvement on the Victorian era and the lives and health of most people in Britain are better as a result. The feudal House of Lords has been reformed, heredity is no longer the only criterion for belonging to this law-making body.

Although the proletariat as Marx described it does not exist in the same way today, people still refer to themselves as 'wage slaves' and debt is becoming a major problem in Britain as many people get caught up in the consumerist society. As Marx predicted, there is also still a huge underclass of the homeless and the unemployed.

Philosophy

Marx is much more relevant to today's world when we look at his philosophy. There are two main philosophical points to be considered:

1 Human nature is not a fixed thing but alters with social and economic conditions. This means that society can be changed by altering the economic system. Nobody was aware of

this before Marx brought it to our attention. However, the history of the twentieth century has shown that it is not as easy as Marx believed to create the society of equals that he thought could develop. The fact that communist states have been riddled with inequalities does not mean that Marx was entirely wrong, but perhaps he was more optimistic about the flexibility of human nature than most people.

2 The most important part of Marx's philosophy was the understanding he gave us about the nature of freedom. Under capitalism we appear to be free but because economic conditions control our work, religion, politics and ideas, we cannot control our lives or society. People are now much more aware of the social and economic influences which shape their lives and this is due, in part, to Marx who first brought it to our attention.

The future

In just 100 years the world has developed in ways that Marx could not have predicted. In the early 1980s, few people could foresee the phenomenal rise of the power of home computers, mobile phones, the Internet; the extent to which technological advances would change aspects of our society in a short space of time. There are signs within the music industry and publishing that people are taking the means of production into their own hands; technology in the Western world means we can all record our own music and make our own books. This will affect the structure of society yet again in ways we cannot be sure of right now.

There is also a growing movement against globalization of industry and exploitation of workers in countries in the developing world. Capitalism has been accused of 'chasing poverty around the world'; as soon as workers in one country receive fair pay and rights then the products become too expensive, and so production is moved to another area of the world. At present in the UK, we are buying in many manufactured goods from China and Laos. This means that the proletariat exists outside our culture and society and becomes almost invisible. Many Marxists are a part of the campaign against globalization, which also includes religious and ecological groups. It is not clear how this will affect society in the long term.

To try to look at the development of Marxism over the next 100 years would be an exercise in science fiction. We cannot predict how technology will change our society. Perhaps work will cease to exist as a result of technological advances, perhaps society will be destroyed by some disaster and we will return to primitive communism.

The revolution Marx predicted never took place, but does that mean it will never happen? The recent global financial crisis and subsequent government spending cuts in many European countries has led to outbreaks of rioting, civil unrest and a resurgence of interest in some of Marx's ideas. Marxists argue that as long as 10 per cent of the population holds 99 per cent of the wealth then there is no equality. There are still numerous Marxist groups in the world who believe that as long as society remains dominated by capitalism, there must be a revolution. As long as the ideas of Marx are still alive in the minds of people throughout the world, this must remain a possibility.